10 DAYS
THAT SHOOK MY WORLD

Searching for My Father
in War-Torn Ethiopia

10 DAYS
THAT SHOOK MY WORLD

Searching for My Father
in War-Torn Ethiopia

Jonathan Wickham

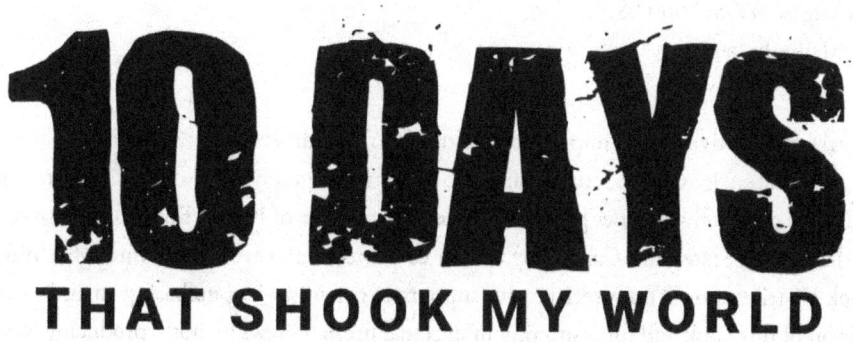

10 DAYS
THAT SHOOK MY WORLD

Searching for My Father
in War-Torn Ethiopia

HISTRIA
PERSPECTIVES

Histria Perspectives

Las Vegas ♦ London ♦ New York ♦ Palm Beach

Published in the United States of America by
Histria Books
7181 N. Hualapai Way, Ste. 130-86
Las Vegas, NV 89166 U.S.A.
HistriaBooks.com

Histria Perspectives is an imprint of Histria Books dedicated to insightful non-fiction books on lifestyle, culture, true crime, politics, and biography that inform, inspire, and challenge perspectives. Titles published under the imprints of Histria Books are distributed in the United States and Canada by Simon & Schuster and worldwide through Unified Book Distribution. We appreciate your support of copyright by purchasing an authorized edition of this book and for respecting intellectual property laws by not reproducing, scanning, or otherwise distributing any part of it by any means without permission. You are supporting authors and enabling Histria Books to continue publishing books for everyone.

All rights reserved. No part of this book may be reprinted or reproduced or utilized in any form or by any electronic, mechanical or other means, now known or hereafter invented, including photocopying and recording, or in any information storage or retrieval system, without the permission in writing from the Publisher. No part of this book may be used or reproduced in any manner for the purpose of training artificial intelligence technologies or systems.

All photos are from the Author's personal collection unless otherwise indicated.

First Edition

Library of Congress Control Number: 2025944902

ISBN 978-1-59211-676-8 (softbound)
ISBN 978-1-59211-704-8 (eBook)

Copyright © 2026 by Jonathan Wickham

For
Marilyn and Zoë
Thank you for all your support
in my Ethiopian adventure and writing about it.
'Ex Africa semper aliquid novi'

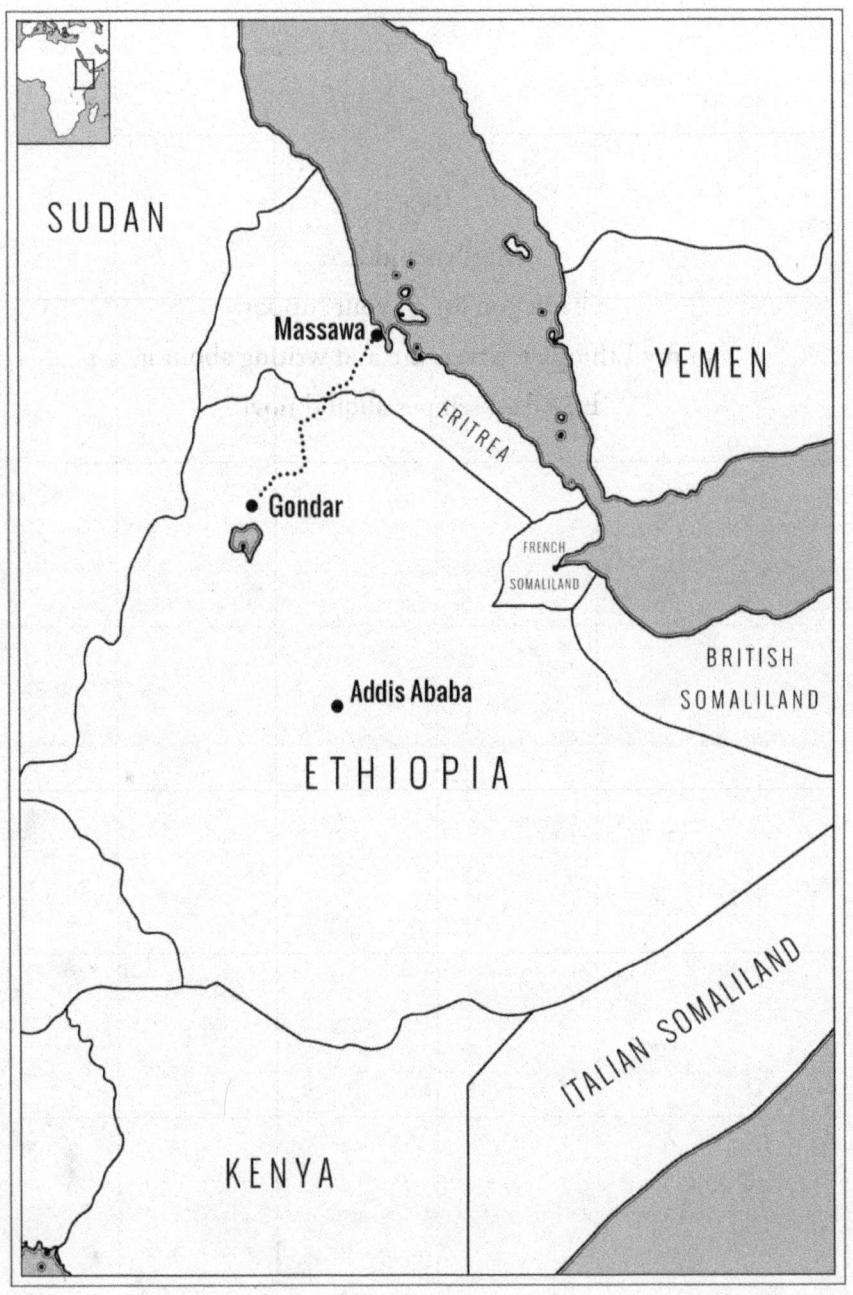

Ethiopia map #1

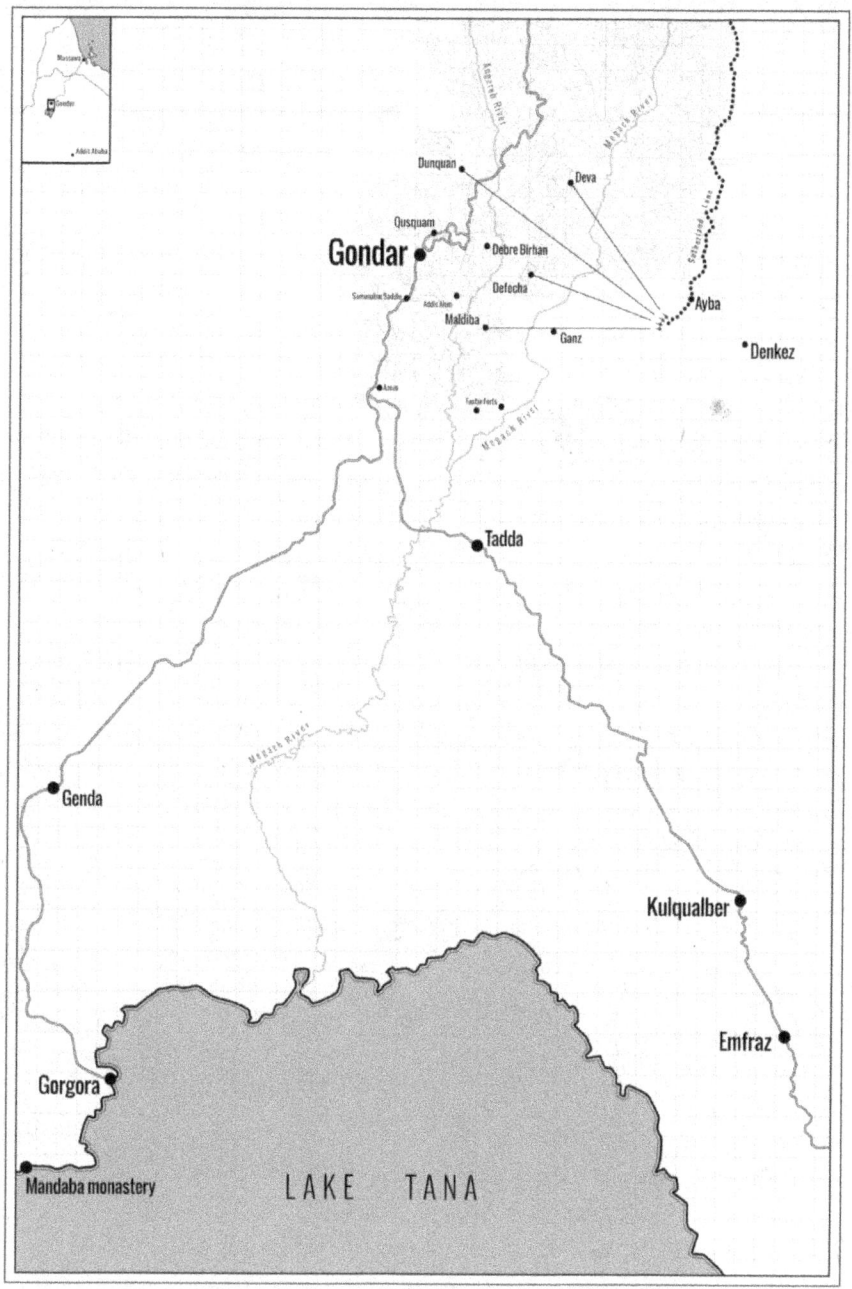

Ethiopia map #2

Contents

Prologue 11

Getting There — 2019-2023 13

DAY ONE — Monday, 3/13/23 29

DAY TWO — Tuesday, 3/14/23 35

DAY THREE — Wednesday, 3/15/23 46

DAY FOUR — Thursday, 3/16/23 55

DAY FIVE — Friday, 3/17/23 65

DAY SIX — Saturday, 3/18/23 79

DAY SEVEN — Sunday, 3/19/23 92

DAY EIGHT — Monday, 3/20/23 99

DAY NINE — Tuesday, 3/21/24 104

DAY TEN — Wednesday 3/22/23 115

Getting It Done — 6/24/23 123

Acknowledgements 137

Appendix 140

54th Nyasaland Artillery Map 147

Select Bibliography 149

About the Author 151

"We were numbed, stunned, because we really hadn't 'taken in' the years of war. For that matter I don't think the world has, even now, 'taken in' the war. In denial are we? Yes. They may put on films as often as they like, usually about Nazis, but the whole world was at war, and whole areas of the conflict have hardly been looked at."

—Doris Lessing, *Alfred and Emily*

"Ethiopia always has a special place in my imagination, and the prospect of visiting Ethiopia attracted me more strongly than a trip to France, England, and America combined. I felt I would be visiting my own genesis, unearthing the roots of what made me an African."

— Nelson Mandela, *Long Walk to Freedom*

Prologue

A pilgrim, I heard someone say recently, is a person who journeys to be transformed. My wife, Marilyn, who's had to come to terms with my three-year obsession, tells me I'm pursuing my heart's desire. She's right, but I put it another way. I feel it's simply something I must do or a vital part of me will begin to disappear.

I've been a documentary filmmaker based in Atlanta, Georgia, for more than 30 years. I've told stories on all kinds of subjects, from English settlers struggling to establish the first American colony at Jamestown, to imagining how a new generation of astronauts could create a colony on the moon. Among those films have been several that explored the different battlegrounds of World War II. From the D-Day landings in Normandy to the carrier battles of the Pacific. As a child born in the 1950s, it was the conflict that I grew up with and which has continued to hold a particular fascination for me. Now I'm about to set off in pursuit of the story that personally connects me to World War II. I'm packing for a trip to a country I've never visited before but where, through one of life's vagaries, my father, as a young man in his early 20s, suddenly found himself transported, thrown into one of the least known battlefronts of history's most bloody and far-flung conflict.

On the bed in front of me are the items I've assembled so far. Clothes, hiking boots, new tropical fedora, electronics, maps, and research materials. Suddenly the question pops into my head — what about taking something from my father? I have his gold signet ring. Would he have worn it then? Probably. His father who he inherited it from was already dead. It has a good motto engraved on it. Audax ero, *I will be bold*. But a better choice would be something military — his bayonet. I might need it. After all I'm going somewhere that until a few months ago was ravaged by a new war.

In his book *Ten Days That Shook the World*,[1] American journalist, John Reed, describes in breathless detail Russia's October Revolution in 1917. In one memorable passage he's hitching a ride to the front with a group of Red Guards. It's the day after a decisive Bolshevik victory over Kerensky's forces outside St. Petersburg. On the way, they're stopped at a checkpoint and Reed is asked to show his press pass. The guards don't recognize what he hands them and, worse still, they're illiterate.

It flashed upon me suddenly; they were going to shoot me!

They stared stupidly at my pass, then at each other.

"It is different from the others," said one, sullenly. "We cannot read, brother."

I took him by the arm. "Come!" I said. "Let's go to that house. Someone there can surely read." They hesitated. "No," said one. The other looked me over. "Why not?" he muttered. "After all, it is a serious crime to kill an innocent man."

Luckily when they knocked on the house door, a frightened woman answered. She came out and, trembling, read aloud what the pass said to the soldiers. Its holder was a journalist, and it was signed by Leon Trotsky.

John Reed didn't get shot that day. And I aim to do the same on my 10-day trip to Ethiopia.

---

[1] John Reed, *Ten Days That Shook The World*, Ch 9, Victory, pp. 299-300.

Getting There — 2019-2023

The genesis of my desire to go to Ethiopia is a discovery I made in June 2019. The summer sun is shining on the flagstone walkway outside and red roses are climbing the pergola that frames it. I'm peering out through a window of the flint cottage that's been my parents' home since they moved back from Africa more than fifty years ago and settled in Norfolk, England. The same house where Winston Churchill was staying when, as first Lord of the Admiralty, he sent the telegram mobilizing the British fleet at the beginning of World War I.

The cottage is in a lovely place, the seaside village of Overstrand. It's just a short walk down to the top of the cliff from where you can look out over the blue grey expanse of the North Sea. The brightness of the day contrasts with my own somber mood. My mother died three days ago. I was in a plane somewhere over the Atlantic when it happened, on my way over from America to see her for what felt like the last time. I was at the counter about to pick up a rental car at Norwich airport when I got my brother David's phone call. In that moment I felt two things — relief followed by profound sinking sadness. I sat down on a bench, completely lost, as I waited for him to arrive. As a friend told me later, "No matter how old you are, you're never really ready to become an orphan."

Now I'm looking for something to hang on to, to persuade myself that my mother is still here. I'm going through a collection of black and white photos that somehow ended up stored inside an old leather bag, like the one doctors used to carry their stethoscope and other instruments in when they made house calls. I'm looking for pictures of my parents' wedding. I remember my mother showing them to me once. In my mind's eye they're large, 6x8. Her parents, or possibly just her mother is standing next to her and my father. But so far all I've found are small 3x4 inch images of their early Africa days.

Then I find an envelope containing some larger pictures, four of them. But these are not of the wedding. The first is of an army truck on a dusty road somewhere in Africa. I can see what look like baobab trees in the background. The driver and his soldier companions are taking a break. But it's the photo underneath the first that really sends a shiver through me. It's of four men in army uniform taken in what looks like a portrait studio. The three in the front row are sitting. The fourth man is standing behind the others. In the middle of the front row is my father. He's wearing a pith helmet, short pants, and a short-sleeved shirt. On his right arm three sergeant's stripes and what looks like a stylized cannon above them. I can't tell for sure because of the bubble texture on the photograph. He's looking straight at the camera…at me, with a slight smile on his face, as if to say, "What took you so long?" It's the first time I've ever seen my father in an army uniform. He and his three companions are looking confidently towards what must have seemed like a big adventure. Four young men going fearlessly off to war. Or maybe not quite. On the floor between my father and his companion in the slouch hat to the right is a bottle whose label reads Bols…Dutch gin to give them Dutch courage?

My father, Bruce Wickham, was always a bit of an enigma to me. He was a charming, easygoing man, guided it seemed by an inner belief that things would work out for the best. But he seldom if ever revealed what led him to have that confidence. The photo with his fellow sergeants I'd unearthed embodies the most mysterious part of my father's life. He'd certainly been in combat but never seemed haunted by any traumatic memories. Like many of his generation, he never told me much about his wartime experience and he died before I had the interest or the opportunity to probe him further. What intrigues me most is that it came when he was 24 years old, an age when many of us make the critical choices which shape our lives.

At 24, I'd been out of college for two years and was living in London. I'd decided teaching wasn't for me and had just bought a Bolex 16mm camera. Working at the London Filmmakers' Coop in Chalk Farm, with an actor friend who also had a talent for mime, I shot, developed and edited a black and white film provocatively titled *The Pleasure Principle*. Somehow with just one character and the help of a bird-mask it explored Freud's theory of how humans instinctively seek pleasure and avoid pain. With that I took my first step on the road to becoming a filmmaker. It may have been a bizarre even risky choice of subject matter, but it didn't endanger my life in any way.

That wasn't the case for my father. He was sent to fight in one of World War II's more obscure and often forgotten theaters, the East Africa campaign. Yet it produced one of the Allies' earliest victories and the liberation of Ethiopia, the first country to be freed from the Axis Powers. Although I didn't yet know how, it had made him a war hero. And afterwards it transformed his life in the most significant ways. It led to a career in Africa, meeting my mother, and to me and my younger brother being born there. As a result, I would spend my first twelve intensely memorable and meaningful years growing up in Africa.

My father's history before the war was more familiar to me but now, I was spurred on to dig deeper. Bruce Wickham was born on Dec. 28, 1916, in the English village of Tarleton, just minutes from the Lancashire coast and an hour's drive north of Liverpool and Manchester, the county's two major cities. His father was a doctor, his mother, the daughter of a successful cotton manufacturer whose company was founded back in the heyday of Britain's Industrial Revolution. Bruce was the oldest of four children. Like many fortunate to be born into the English upper middle class, life was relatively good to him, even growing up in the years of the Great Depression. He got a scholarship to Pembroke College, Cambridge, where, on the advice of his favorite uncle, Tommy, who had also been his teacher, he studied the Classics. Tommy Brown had been an artillery lieutenant in World War I and had survived despite being severely wounded just a month after arriving at the Western Front. Doubtless he influenced my father's decision to join the artillery section of the Officer Training Corps during his time at Cambridge. But when it came to choosing a career, Bruce Wickham seems to have trusted his own instinct. If he was good at Latin and Greek, why not learn a living language, something African maybe like Swahili or even Chinyanja? In his final year at college, he planned to apply for a position in the Colonial Service which would take him to some part of the increasingly rickety but still sprawling British empire. Then just days before Christmas 1938, about to turn 22 and with graduation only six months away, he was hit by the first of two major losses. His mother died of cancer. Two months later, his father died from a burst appendix.

Meanwhile, the political crisis that had long been threatening to destroy peace in Europe finally came to a head. On September 3, 1939, Bruce Wickham and the rest of Britain heard prime minister Neville Chamberlain solemnly announce on the radio that Britain was at war with Nazi Germany. The world turned upside down, all bets for a rosy future somewhere in Britain's empire seemed suddenly off.

A few months after I flew home to Atlanta, I had a dream about my father, the first in several years. It started in a familiar way; he's back after a long trip he's made somewhere to improve his failing health. But this time I hear him speaking to me. He tells me, "I'm an odd bird. I'm caught between two worlds. But that's the way I am." This unexpected and disquietingly vivid 'encounter' seemed like a call to action. As one of my favorite history writers, Tony Horwitz, once described his creative process: "Half my research is going to where the history really happened." It was time to solve my father's deepest mystery, and to do that required going to Ethiopia.

Monday, January 20th, 2020, is an auspicious day to begin. It's both Martin Luther King Day and the day Ethiopian Christians celebrate Epiphany. I'm driving out along Memorial Drive, the highway which goes all the way to Stone Mountain, Georgia's spectacular natural wonder. The monolithic piece of granite rises like a giant whale above the pine forests that surrounds it. One side of its gray flanks is scarred by a carving of Jefferson Davis, Robert E. Lee, and Stonewall Jackson, the Confederate trilogy. Georgians are now wrestling with what to do about it. But today I'm not going that far. After a few miles, I pull into a strip mall which has seen better days. Now it's the proud new home of the Ethiopian Community Association of Atlanta. An estimated 20,000[2] Ethiopians make their home in Georgia, most of them in the Atlanta metro area. Inside I meet Tegist Borga, a woman dressed elegantly in white with several gold rings on her fingers who's come here directly from the Epiphany service. Epiphany, I learn, is different for Ethiopians. Instead of the arrival of the Three Wise Men it's the day when they celebrate the baptism of Jesus by John the Baptist. One of the biggest celebrations is held in the Gondar. That's a happy coincidence, because one of the few details I know about my father's wartime service is that's the city where he fought. "Can you put me in contact with some people from Gondar?" She frowns for a moment thinking. Just then the front door opens, and a young man comes in. "Ah, he will

---

[2] Migration Policy Institute, RAD Diaspora Profile 'The Ethiopian Diaspora in the United States' July 2014 p. 5.

know," she says, introducing me to Samson Tegegne. He immediately starts thumbing through contacts on his phone and pulls up the name of someone who will play a key role in my quest to get to Ethiopia — Dr. Haile Larebo, professor of history at Morehouse College.

An hour or so later, I'm looking at his photo on the Morehouse website. He's wearing black rimmed glasses, a bright yellow polka dot tie, and a welcoming smile. Haile, it turns out, is the author of a book about Mussolini's empire building attempt in Ethiopia,[3] in which Gondar figured prominently. Although he isn't from the city, he's spent time there at the university, he tells me when we talk a few days later. He puts me in touch with a friend and Gondar native who will turn out to be my second key contact. Mulatu Wubneh is a retired professor of environmental and urban planning at East Carolina University who now lives in Silver Springs, Maryland. "I came here on a scholarship before the Derg came to power. I didn't return because of the chaos that followed." The Derg was the Marxist military regime that overthrew the longtime emperor of Ethiopia, Haile Selassie, in 1974 and probably murdered him a year later. Over the course of several phone calls and meetings on Zoom, Mulatu paints a stark picture of what life in Gondar was like in the fall of 1941, during the final days of the Italian occupation. "Food had become scarce and very expensive. As the British bombing intensified and the fighting on the ground kept getting closer, my parents, like many, began to fear for their lives and fled the city."

The Saturday after my visit to the Ethiopian Community Association, I'm out with two of my running club buddies, Stan and Bill. We're a mile into our usual 10-mile route, passing through the towering forest next to the Botanical Gardens and about to enter the wide expanse of Piedmont Park, in Atlanta's Midtown, when I find myself blurting out, "Guess what guys, I'm planning a trip to Ethiopia." Being avid runners, their first question naturally is, "What's the race?" "The race?" I say hesitantly, "I guess to run in my father's footsteps." Stan is skeptical about whether this is a good idea. "Isn't that where there are still landmines going off?" He says he'll check with some Ethiopian friends of his up in Washington DC where he lived until recently. The following week he tells me they give the trip a

---

[3] Haile Larebo, 'The Building of an Empire: Italian Land Policy and Practice in Ethiopia, 1935-1941,' 2006.

thumbs up. Their endorsement isn't all together surprising. After all, Abiy Ahmed, Ethiopia's prime minister, had recently received the Nobel Peace Prize for ending the country's long running war with neighboring Eritrea. In his acceptance speech in Oslo, he emphasized the need for reconciliation, at both the political and the personal level. "For you to have a peaceful night, your neighbor must have a peaceful night as well."[4]

Six weeks later the Covid-19 pandemic hits. We're in lockdown. It doesn't look like I'll be going anywhere further than the grocery store for a quite a while. As a documentary filmmaker I'm not considered an essential worker, so all activity on that front comes to a screeching halt. The enforced break from my normal routine does provide one important benefit, it gives me time to dig deeper into my father's missing World War II history. The most critical piece of information I need to find to get started is the name of his unit.

One of the few things my father had told me about his war experience was that he served in the artillery. Back in 2016, I'd requested his service record from the British Ministry of Defense. When a brown envelope arrived, I opened it in eager anticipation. The contents at first seemed promising. I learned that in the same month that war broke out, my father had signed up to become an officer cadet in the Royal Artillery in Cambridge, where he'd just graduated. Over the course of 1940 his training progressed until in October, when now promoted from private to lance bombardier, the artillery equivalent of lance corporal, he was sent to Yeovil in Somerset to begin training to fire a Bofors anti-aircraft gun. By then air defense was the country's top priority. The Luftwaffe had launched its deadly campaign to bomb Britain into submission first by day in the Battle of Britain and then by night in raids commonly known as "The Blitz." A wartime training film showed me how he and his fellow gun layer would have learned to work as a team, rapidly aligning their horizontal and vertical gunsights to shoot down a fast-moving enemy aircraft. But then the trail went cold. In December 1940, the last entry in his military record read "Discharged, his services being no longer required on proceeding

---

[4] Abiy Ahmed, 'Nobel Prize Lecture,'Olso, 2019. https://www.nobelprize.org/prizes/peace/2019/abiy/lecture/

overseas." No mention of where or to what unit. I had to find another way forward.

I knew that most of the British forces sent to Ethiopia were part of the Kings African Rifles infantry battalions. Known by their acronym KAR, these battalions were made up of African troops from all over East Africa — Kenya, Uganda, Tanzania and Nyasaland, now Malawi, where my father would ultimately work after the war and where I was born. So perhaps his artillery unit was part of the KAR. As I delved into the definitive history of the KAR by Hubert Moyse-Bartlett, I discovered that the 2/2 KAR battalion, a newly formed infantry unit from Nyasaland, was sent to fight at Gondar. The initial plan was for them to attack along the modern road Italian engineers had built with Ethiopian labor and which threads its way through the towering mountains to the North into the city. But, he writes ominously, "The whole position was extensive, obscure and well-defended." A successful attack would require strength in the one element the campaign chronically lacked — artillery.

At which point, Moyse-Bartlett writes, "a delay occurred while the new 25-pounder guns of 54 (Ny) Field Battery were awaited."[5] It took me a few moments to parse that cryptic sentence. 'Ny' I recognized was the abbreviation for 'Nyasaland'. Then I remembered a comment my mother had made many years ago about my father which had always puzzled me, "People thought he was in the KAR but he wasn't." Sergeant Bruce Wickham must in fact have been assigned to the 54th Nyasaland Field Battery. I'd uncovered the first important key in my search for my father.

But it wouldn't unlock anything until the Covid lockdown loosened. The records that I needed to look at hadn't been digitized. They were only available as physical copies kept at the British National Archives which remained firmly closed. In early September 2020, I contact Simon Mills, a friend I'd met during filming for a documentary about the Britannic, Titanic's less famous sister ship, which also sank but in the shallower and warmer waters of the Mediterranean, in the channel between the Greek mainland and the island of Kea. Amazingly, Simon actually owns the shipwreck of Britannic but more importantly for me he lives on the west

---

[5] Lt. Col. Hubert Moyse-Bartlett, 'The King's African Rifles,' Vol. 2, Ch 21, pp. 146-147/560 Available at Google Books.

side of London near the National Archives at Kew Gardens, and when they reopen, he manages to snag one of the first research appointments. A couple of days later, he emails me a trove of documents. They include the 54th Nyasaland War Diary and — most astonishing of all — the artillery map used by my father's unit during the assault on Gondar on Nov. 27, 1941. You can actually see the holes punched in it so that it could be attached to a board where the gun crew could see it. It becomes my "treasure map." Literally my guide to following in my father's footsteps. But just as the Covid pandemic restrictions begin to ease a bit, things take a turn for the worse in Ethiopia.

Because of Covid, prime minister Abiy Ahmed decides to postpone elections due to take place in August 2020. The disgruntled leaders of the Tigray People's Liberation Front (TPLF), the party of the Tigray region who actually supported Abiy's rise to power, see this move as a betrayal and refuse to go along. In defiance, they hold their own local election. Abiy responds by cutting off funds to the region. In early November 2020, tensions between the region and the central government erupt into outright war. With support from Eritrea, Ethiopia's neighbor who Abiy made peace with, his National Defense Force scores a quick victory, capturing the Tigrayan capital of Mekele. But by July 2021, the tables are turned. TPLF forces retake Mekele and forge on south towards Addis Ababa. They reach Dessie only eight hours from the capital and enter Lalibela whose famous rock-hewn churches make it a top tourist destination. There a counter-offensive by federal forces and regional militias, supported by a timely infusion of armed drones supplied by Turkey, Iran, and the United Arab Emirates, stops the Tigrayans dead in their tracks. Quickly they fall back and by early 2022 the struggle reaches a stalemate. All the while there are reports of growing starvation, refugees fleeing, and atrocities against civilians inflicted by both sides. The prospects for my going to Ethiopia continue to look bleak.

During this time of hoping and waiting, I read Toni Morrison's novel, *Song of Solomon*. I quickly became fascinated by the main character Milkman Dead's efforts to track down his African American and even African roots. Eventually his pursuit leads him to Virginia where he witnesses a group of children performing their whirling dance and singing about Solomon, an enslaved ancestor who possesses an extraordinary power. Milkman has a revelation: "He could fly! You hear me? My great-grandaddy could fly! Goddamn!" He finally surrenders to the possibility of having that power himself. And it's a power he desperately needs. In the book's final scene, as he hurls himself off a precipice in the direction of his best friend, Guitar, who he believes is trying to kill him, he is buoyed up by a single thought: "If you surrendered to the air, you could *ride* it."[6]

Even though I'm a white guy, I was born in Africa and feel myself irresistibly drawn to the idea of the Flying African who takes off to return to a lost home or at least die trying. It reminds me of the story I heard as a child growing up. It was told to me by Nickson Ndau, a man who worked for my family and taught me how to make my first catapult, what Americans call a slingshot, among other useful and practical skills. Nickson's story is a coming-of-age saga. One day Hlakanyana, a young boy, finds a yam while playing in the vegetable garden outside his house. He brings it to his mother who promises to cook it for him. But then, mmm… it smells so good, she can't help eating it herself. When her son returns, she's filled with remorse, so she gives him a beautiful clay pot. It's the first of a series of progressively more useful and meaningful gifts Hlakanyana receives from the people he encounters during his ensuing wanderings through the surrounding countryside. At the end he sings — and I always hear Nickson's voice singing the words: "See me, Hlakanyana, with me my spear, the spear which the olde man gave me, the olde man who tore my blanket, the blanket which the woodcutters gave me…." And so it goes on, recounting each gift and its giver. Now he's ready to face whatever life has in store for him.

When I went back to Africa for the first time after 25 years, the emotional high point of the trip was tracking down Nickson in his village in Malawi. He was an old man by then and I felt like Hlakanyana being reunited with him. This trip to follow in my father's footsteps feels similarly charged with meaning and emotion. So, like Milkman, I imagine myself soaring into the air. All I need to do is keep heading East across the vast Atlantic Ocean.

***

The in-flight screen in front of me shows our itinerary with the plane icon approaching the Portuguese coast. The food trolley draws level with my seat and the

---

[6] Toni Morrison, 'Song of Solomon', 1977, p. 507 & p. 515.

flight attendant's voice asks whether I'd like, "Chicken or beef?" During dinner we pass over Portugal and Spain, heading towards the blue expanse of the Mediterranean. It's Sunday, March 12, 2023, I'm aboard Ethiopian Airlines flight 501 from Washington Dulles to Addis Ababa. What changed to make it possible? Two things: in October 2022, my friend Mulatu Wubneh called to let me know he was off to start teaching a semester at the University of Gondar and on November 3rd, the Ethiopian Government and the TPLF signed a ceasefire agreement which appears to be holding.

I'm not making the trip alone. About a month before departure I texted Scott Engel, a friend of mine who I know has a taste for exotic travel. Some years ago, we'd been to Egypt together on a scouting trip for a documentary film I was researching. "I know this is short notice," I wrote, "but if you want to find out more about James Bruce, his search for source of the Nile and how he came across the long-lost Book of Enoch, this is your chance." His reply came back immediately, "When can we meet?"

Scott designs and makes picture frames for a living — I have one in which a photo of the two of us standing inside the cavernous stone interior of Egypt's Great Pyramid is surrounded by a border of miniature golden pyramids. He's also spent much of his life pursuing esoteric knowledge and mysteries. He's traveled to Tibet and hosted South American shamans performing ceremonies at home in Georgia. He's well acquainted with Ethiopia's longstanding claim to be the home of the Ark of the Covenant but he admitted, like most people, to being profoundly ignorant of the part the country played in World War II.

With hours to fill on our flight to Addis Ababa, I lay out the basics. In October 1935, after months of build-up and threats, Mussolini's Italian forces invaded. His Fascist dream was to combine Ethiopia, Eritrea, and Somalia into a new Italian empire stretching, across the Horn of Africa. By May 1936, after putting up a spirited but almost suicidal resistance against Italy's superior weapons, including poison gas attacks from the air which recalled the horrors of World War I, Ethiopian Emperor, Haile Selassie, was forced to flee his country. The following month in Geneva he delivered an impassioned plea for justice at a meeting of the League of Nations: "I ask the fifty-two nations, who have given the Ethiopian people a promise to help them in their resistance to the aggressor, what are they willing to do for Ethiopia?"⁷ Ethiopia was in fact one of the founding members and the only country from Africa in this precursor of the United Nations. But Haile Selassie's appeal fell on deaf ears. Britain and France were afraid that providing any kind of aid to Ethiopia might set off a new world war. Still Haile Selassie's speech was widely reported in the press and carried on radio. It would have been the first time my father, then in his final year at school, along with the vast majority of the British public had ever heard words spoken by an African leader. In the United States, more than 1,000 New York policemen were called out to deal with pitched battles between African Americans and Italian Americans breaking out in Harlem. 500 African Americans even went so far as to volunteer to fight for Haile Selassie.⁸ But Ethiopia was left to resist on its own. One event during the subsequent Italian occupation illustrates the level of brutality Mussolini's forces were prepared to unleash to drive the Ethiopian people into submission. In February 1937, as a reprisal for a failed assassination attempt on the Italian Viceroy Graziani, at least 18,000 Ethiopians were massacred.⁹

When World War II broke out, Mussolini at first held back, keeping Italy neutral. But then seeing the rapid success of Hitler's Blitzkrieg and not wishing to miss out on the spoils, in June 1940 he declared war on Britain and France, hoping to gain more land, especially in Africa. His first target was the British territories adjoining his new East African empire. Initially caught off guard and outnumbered, it took the British several months to gather their forces and devise a plan to strike back. They began advancing on three fronts. Conventional forces attacked from Sudan in the north and from Kenya by way of Somalia in the south. At the same time a third group began to stealthily infiltrate their way into Ethiopia from the

---

[7] Haile Selassie's appeal to the League of Nations, May 12, 1936 from Black Past. https://www.blackpast.org/global-african-history/1936-emperor-haile-selassie-ethiopia-appeal-league-nations/

[8] Ruth Ben-Ghiat, 'When Harlem and Little Italy Clashed over Ethiopia' 6/8/2021 https://lucid.substack.com/p/when-harlem-and-little-italy-clashed

Rachel Maddow Deja News Episode 6: "Hello America, this is Addis Ababa." 7/24/2023

https://rachel-maddow-presents-deja-news.simplecast.com/episodes/episode-6-hello-america-this-is-addis-ababa

[9] Jeff Pearce, 'Prevail: The Inspiring Story of Ethiopia's Victory over Mussolini's Invasion,' 2014 p. 397.

West. It was led by Major Orde Wingate, a military maverick who would later make a name for himself leading a special operations unit behind Japanese lines in the jungles of Burma. As Gen. Archibald Wavell, his commanding officer, described him, "Few people looked more like a fiery leader of partisans than Wingate." He led a small but highly trained guerrilla force made up of Ethiopian exiles, Sudanese regulars and assorted Europeans. The latter, in the words of one historian, were "men who disliked the formal side of regimental life or were merely bored with garrison duty and in search of adventure."[10] Wingate's mission was to pave the way for the return of exiled Emperor Haile Selassie. His primary tactic for achieving this was to link up with the *Arbegnoch*, the Ethiopian Patriot fighters, already launching sporadic attacks against Italian garrisons in the Eastern regions of Gojjam and Amhara. Eventually, as I would discover, Wingate's inspired use of Patriot fighters alongside regular British forces would play a critical role in the final phase of the campaign in Gondar.

The fight for Ethiopia turned into the first British success story. By April 1941, using forces made up primarily of African and Indian regiments, the British entered the capital, Addis Ababa. By then they had occupied much of the South and East of the country as well as Eritrea which gave them vital access to the Red Sea. In the west Wingate's small guerrilla army, that he called Gideon Force after the biblical hero who defeated the Midianite hordes, had with Patriot support overcome much larger Italian garrisons. On May 5th, riding a white horse, he led Emperor Haile Selassie's triumphant motorcade back into Addis Ababa.[11]

But there's one major holdout, the Amhara region in the northern highlands. Its main city is Gondar, Ethiopia's old imperial capital with castles and palaces dating back to the 17th century. Today, online tour operators call it the Camelot of Africa. Mussolini orders his most talented field commander and now also provincial governor, Gen. Guglielmo Nasi, to use his remaining 40,000 men, composed of European and Ethiopian troops as well as a strong force of artillery, to

---

[10] Andrew Stewart, 'The First Victory: The Second World War and the East Africa Campaign' 2016, Ch 9, p. 192.

[11] David Shirreff, 'Bare Feet and Bandoliers: Wingate, Sandford, the Patriots and the Liberation of Ethiopia,' 2009, p. 186.

fight on. Already his German ally, Field Marshal Rommel, known as the 'Desert Fox', leading his elite Afrika Korps has succeeded in driving the British forces out of Libya and is threatening Egypt, the key to Britain's hold on the Mediterranean, the Suez Canal and North Africa. If Rommel succeeds and Egypt falls the British will be forced to abandon Ethiopia and Mussolini's dream of an empire in the Horn of Africa can live again.[12] Maj. General C.C. Fowkes, commander of British Forces in Ethiopia has other ideas.

Known as "Fluffy" to his white officers and "Bwana Box" to his African troops, on account of his folksy charm, Fowkes is a harsh taskmaster. "Straight and hard at the enemy and keep on going," is his motto. But to pull off this mission he'll need to beef up his artillery strength. Without it his task of defeating General Nasi in Gondar will be a bloody if not impossible one. True Fowkes has the advantage of superior airpower, but his ground forces, composed mainly of African troops, are fewer, and Gondar is a natural fortress accessible only through narrow mountain passes to the south and especially to the north where General Nasi has concentrated the bulk of his men and his biggest guns.[13]

According to the 54th Nyasaland Field Battery's War Diary, on September 30, 1941, after a grueling 1,300 miles by truck from Zomba, Nyasaland's capital, Sgt. Bruce Wickham along with six other white NCOs arrives in Nairobi, Kenya. It's one of only two specific references the War Diary makes to my father.[14] Nairobi may well be where the photo that originally sparked my investigation was taken. The second photo of the military truck probably records a rest stop somewhere along the dusty miles between Kenya and Nyasaland, today Malawi. He'd arrived there barely two months before, after another long and hazardous trip from Britain, first by naval convoy through the Atlantic Ocean and then overland by train, which brought him for the first time to the heart of Africa.

In spite of the outbreak of war, it turns out that Bruce Wickham had still managed to stick to his original plan to pursue a career overseas. Foreseeing that Britain

---

[12] Angelo Del Boca, 'Gli Italiani in Africa Orientale' Vol. 3 La caduta dell' impero, p. 508; David Shirreff, 'Bare Feet and Bandoliers' Ch. 8, p. 226.

[13] Lt. Col. Hubert Moyse-Bartlett, 'The King's African Rifles, Vol. 2,' Ch. 21, p. 145.

[14] 54th War Diary of 54th Nyasaland Field Battery, Sept. 30, 1941, UK National Archives WO 169/2980 1941 Aug.-Dec. (See Appendix).

would soon be fighting on many fronts, including Africa, the Colonial Service and the War Office had struck a deal. Candidates could still apply for overseas posts "provided that an individual needed by the army should be instantly released," and that "no recruit would be sent abroad until he had done three to six months military training."[15] This explains my father's sudden discharge from the Royal Artillery once he'd completed training on the Bofors anti-aircraft gun. He arrives in Nyasaland fully expecting to begin working as a junior administrative officer in one of the country's more rural districts. But a man called Bingham has a very different idea.

"Well, I come of a military family. We've been soldiers for several generations now," says a voice in plummy upper-class tones. Major Francis Bingham, as I discovered listening to his oral history at the Imperial War Museum, had been put in charge of forming a new artillery unit for immediate deployment in Ethiopia.[16] In late May 1941 he'd arrived by plane in Nyasaland, where he'd once served in the military and then later in the colonial service. He would have known that the original two battalions of the King's African Rifles were formed here in the 1890s. In the wars that followed, most notably the World War I campaign against the Germans in East Africa, they gained the reputation as fierce fighters, to some the Gurkhas of Africa. There at the KAR headquarters he finds the latest crop of African recruits who have just completed nine months of basic training. As Bingham recalls: "I think they were thoroughly bored and looking for a bit of excitement. To see another country, hear the sound of guns actually firing off appealed to their imagination." What Bingham is offering is beyond these young soldiers' wildest dreams. The 55 recruits he selects will be the first to become part of an artillery unit. They'd be learning how to fire guns bigger than any they'd ever seen.

At the same time, Bingham's contacts in the white civil administration must have tipped him off to the recent arrival from England of a new district officer

---

[15] Sir Ralph Furse, [Father of the Modern Colonial Service] 'Aucuparius: Recollections of a Recruiting Officer', 1962,

[16] Maj. Francis H. Bingham Oral History, Cat. No. 3939, Imperial War Museum, London. https://www.iwm.org.uk/collections/item/object/80003923

named Bruce Wickham. This young man had already mastered the skills the artillery commander so urgently needed — how to operate a field gun and how to command a gun crew. Coincidentally my father had learned those skills in Yeovil, Somerset, very close to Bath where Emperor Haile Selassie had lived in exile. And the emperor and the young lance bombardier had something else in common. Shortly before fleeing his country, Haile Selassie had stood on the front lines at Dessie, 300 miles north of his capital, Addis Ababa. There he'd put on his helmet and started firing an Oerlikon 37mm anti-aircraft gun, one of only two his country possessed, as Italian planes swooped down to attack the Ethiopian positions.[17]

Maj. Bingham immediately drafts Bruce Wickham as a sergeant in the 54th Nyasaland Field Battery. On the same day that that my father arrives in Nairobi, rumor becomes reality, according to the War Diary. Bingham is officially informed that the size of his artillery unit will be doubled, from 4-guns to 8-guns, equipped with the British Army's newest and best field weapon. Bingham scrambles, quickly commandeering a section of Kenyan gunners and their white officer to add to his Nyasaland contingent. While he continues the hunt for truck drivers, signalers, and other personnel, Bingham gives Sgt. Wickham his first assignment, sending him down to the port of Mombasa on the Kenyan coast to help organize the motor transport they'll need.[18] The 54th Nyasaland Field Battery has less than two months to assemble the added guns and manpower that General Fowkes badly needs if he's to succeed in dislodging General Nasi and his forces from the last Italian-held fortress in Gondar.

***

By now the itinerary map on my in-flight screen is showing Ethiopian Airlines flight 501 making its way down the Red Sea. Soon we'll be crossing back over land, over the Tigray region where November's ceasefire agreement brought two years of bitter fighting to at least a temporary halt. By some estimates as many as 600,000 people had died by then, most of them civilians, the victims of starvation

---

[17] Jeff Pierce, 'Prevail: The Inspiring Story of Ethiopia's Victory over Mussolini's Invasion,' Ch. 10, p. 204.

[18] War Diary of 54th Nyasaland Field Battery, Oct. 4, 1941, (See Appendix).

and genocide. The map soon shows us passing Gondar, only 100 miles below the Tigray border, and heading on towards Addis Ababa.

At noon on Oct. 29, 1941, Bruce Wickham and the 54th Nyasaland dock in Massawa, the recently liberated Eritrean port on the Red Sea. The 300 men, along with their trucks and ammunition, have landed only to discover, as Maj. Bingham puts it, that "my guns hadn't arrived yet…they were in a ship that had been wandering about in the Indian Ocean somewhere." They'll have to wait two more weeks for the ship carrying their eight new 25-pounders, the British Army's state-of-the-art field artillery piece, to arrive. Then they'll make a mad dash through Tigray, the same area in which Ethiopia's latest war has barely ended, arriving a few miles north of Gondar on the night of November 16.

The final assault on the city will begin in 10 days, the same number of days that I have to track down my father's movements and to relive and better understand how his Ethiopian experience affected and shaped him. At the same time, I have become progressively aware through the long months of preparation that this will be a journey of discovery for me too. It's been eight years since I last made a trip to Africa. I'm no longer a young man like my father was when he came here, which means my interests in this country are much broader than his would have been. I intend to get to know more about Ethiopia, to learn its deeper history extending back well before World War II and from there all the way forward to the still turbulent present. Like a pilgrim, I hope to be transformed and invigorated with fresh insights and understanding by this journey into an unknown land.

DAY ONE — Monday, 3/13/23

At 7am local time, Ethiopian Airlines flight 501 begins making its descent. The Great Rift Valley that slices through Ethiopia's highlands comes into view through the window. Its floor is dotted with silvery lakes in the early morning sun. For a moment I imagine the Rift's long gash tearing on down through two-thirds of the African continent until, in its final 300-mile stretch, it fills with another lake where I went swimming as a child — Lake Malawi. And to the west of it lies the country's capital, Lilongwe, where I was born. Pulling my attention back to where we are now, I see straggling down from the still shadow-covered mountains on the northern side of the Rift an immense expanse of buildings that is Addis Ababa, now home to close to 5.5 million people. And then we touch down at Bole International airport where it seems Ethiopian Airlines is by far the dominant carrier. I only count a handful of other planes, from the Gulf and Saudi Arabia, as we taxi in.

Going through passport control and immigration is uneventful. The customs officer is indifferent to my certificate showing a negative Covid test. It's almost a disappointment after all the effort I put into avoiding crowds and indoor events over the past two weeks. Apparently, no one is concerned anymore about catching the virus. I'd probably feel the same if I lived in a country that until a few months ago was at war with itself. And however tenuous the peace still may be, I had decided in the end it wasn't a good idea to bring my father's bayonet with me.

It takes a while for my bag to show up on the carousel. I'm amazed at the enormous size and number of bags many of the Ethiopian passengers have brought with them. I imagine it's because they've been a way a while or are bringing back presents for family and friends. The Ethiopian diaspora has grown tremendously in the past 50 years. My friend Mulatu, who left in the early 1970s, is one of the estimated 250,000 Ethiopians who live in the Washington DC area alone. Wrangling all the luggage onto carts keeps a small army of porters busy. Every now and then I glance over at an American woman who I recognize as having checked in at the same time as me at Dulles airport in Washington. I'm reassured to see she's still waiting for her bag too. Meanwhile, Scott has gone to change some money.

Eventually, my large green roller bag shows up and we make our way over to the domestic terminal. It's a little shabby and bare still. The extensive airport renovation that's going on hasn't reached here yet. But there's an inviting coffee and snack area with hand-crafted wooden furniture and colorful rugs. We still have a couple of hours to wait for our Gondar flight. By now jet lag has dulled my brain. But Scott has the perfect antidote. He begins telling me a story about Ethiopia's most famous and controversial treasure — the Ark of the Covenant. It comes from Graham Hancock, the journalist and now author of a provocative theory about how this elusive object came to Ethiopia and what it actually is.

The story told in *Kebra Nagast* — The Glory of Kings, Ethiopia's national epic — is that around 950BC, King Solomon and Sheba, the Ethiopian Queen who visited him, had a romantic encounter. On her return to Ethiopia, Sheba gave birth to their son, Menelik I. When Menelik reached adulthood, he wanted to meet his father and so traveled to Jerusalem. After a year he felt he'd absorbed enough of Solomon's wisdom and that it was time to come home. But he also decided to take with him something of immense value. Through a clever piece of subterfuge, he and his entourage, many of them high ranking Jews assigned by Solomon himself, managed to smuggle the Ark of the Covenant out of Israel and take it back to Ethiopia where it has remained ever since. Most archaeologists, says Hancock, dismiss this claim, preferring to believe the Ark was taken by the Babylonians when they sacked the temple in Jerusalem in 587BC. But Hancock favors a third possibility. It's the story he heard from the Beth Israel community, the Jews of Ethiopia, once known as the Falasha meaning "wanderers." They originally lived in Egypt, on the Island of Elephantine on the Nile. There they built a temple around 650BC. And since the Old Testament states that one the primary purposes of the temple in Jerusalem is to house the Ark, Hancock believes that this temple on the Nile became its new home when the Jewish King Mennaseh turned to pagan idolatry. Not wanting to see the Ark defiled, loyal priests spirited it out of the country. It remained in Elephantine until around 400BC when the Jewish community's practice of animal sacrifice, specifically the killing of rams, brought them into violent conflict with local Egyptians who worshipped the ram-god, Knum.

Taking the Ark with them, the Jews fled south along the course of Nile until it brought them to its source, Lake Tana, in Ethiopia. There the Ark remained until around 300AD when Ezanas, the first Ethiopian king to convert to Christianity, brought it to his capital, Axum, in present day Tigray, where it is still housed today.

In the course of unraveling this story, Hancock was particularly struck by the descriptions of the Ark of the Covenant. The dimensions were very specific, as well as the materials it was to be made of, wood and gold. And there were these two mysterious tablets which it contained. It sounded to him like a blueprint for a piece of technology. But what he admits makes people suspicious of this tale is that no one apart from the single monk, who is appointed to guard the Ark, is allowed to see it. Over the course of the 10 years Hancock spent researching the history of the Ark, he talked to several of these monks who acted as its guardians, inside a special building next to the church of Mary of Zion in Axum where it is now kept, surrounded by armed men. Each of the guardian monks, he says, first developed cataracts, then went blind and died within two years. When he asked them what was causing this, they each said it was the Ark, which is "a thing of fire." The conclusion Hancock reaches is that the Ark is a lost piece of technology and, like decaying nuclear fuel, seems capable of emitting some deadly form of radiation. For that reason alone, it's worth keeping out of sight and out of mind in Ethiopia. In fact, when he teasingly asked the Israeli ambassador there why he didn't send agents from Mossad "to grab it," the man looked him straight in the eye and said, "That's the very last thing we'd want to do. For the Ark to be re-introduced into Israel right now would be a catastrophe for the world."

At 10:15 am, I'm roused from Scott's mesmerizing excursion. They're calling our flight to Gondar. As we and our fellow passengers board a bus, we get our first brief taste of Africa that awaits us outside. A flock of exotic-looking and unfamiliar birds are perched in a nearby tree. The bus deposits us on the tarmac beside our waiting plane. It's a turbo prop De Havilland, seating about 70 people. The plane is made in Canada but originally the company started in the UK. It built one of the most famous British planes of World War II, the De Havilland Mosquito fighter bomber. Growing up in Malawi I remember gluing together an Airfix model of one and carefully painting camouflage on its wings. Before I was even aware that my father had fought in World War II, the subject had already captured my imagination like most young boys of my generation. I devoured the comics from War Picture Library depicting actual battles where Germans yelled "Feuer" and Japanese screamed "Banzai." Later these gave way to cinematic depictions like *The Guns of Navarone* and *The Great Escape*. Eventually I made films of my own, a documentary about an American destroyer mysteriously sunk off the beaches of Normandy during the D-Day landings and another about the aircraft carrier USS Hornet which launched the B-25 bombers of Doolittle Raid on Tokyo, Roosevelt's revenge against Imperial Japan for Pearl Harbor. Traveling now in a plane with such a strong wartime pedigree seems like the perfect way to start my Gondar World War II expedition.

After takeoff, we still stay low enough to see the contours of land as we fly northwest back into the heart of the Ethiopia's northern highlands. It brings back memories of the DC-3, another World War II-era prop plane that I flew in from Malawi to Zimbabwe to go to boarding school. Fortunately, this flight only lasts an hour. There's none of the turbulence I used to dread and which kept me from eating the delicious asparagus-topped lunches the flight attendants plied us with for fear of getting 'air sick.' In no time through one of the windows on the opposite side of the plane I catch sight of the blue green expanse of the Lake Tana, source of the Blue Nile. After the hours I spent on Google Earth in preparation for this trip the landscape almost seems like somewhere I've been and know already. There's less greenery than I expected, the mountains are yellow and brown. But that makes sense. This is now the height of the dry season. After skirting the eastern shore of Lake Tana, we begin descending. I start to make out some details, the round shapes of church roofs, usually blue or pink, with a halo of green forest surrounding them. And then we're coming in to land at the southern end of Gondar, now a city of some 400,000 people. During World War II less than a tenth of that number lived here.

The airport is unexpectedly beautiful, palm trees out front with arches above the windows and a row of stone battlements along the roof. It's dedicated to Emperor Tewodros. His golden statue stands out in front of the parking lot where Scott and I find the promised shuttle from the Gondar Plaza Hotel waiting for us. As we drive off, I spot the shells of two concrete buildings. Intuitively I know that I'm looking at surviving remnants of the Italian occupation. On the drive into town I start to see some of the familiar sights of Africa. Acacia trees and eucalyptus groves, a boy with a herd of goats, holding a stick across his shoulders, women carrying pots and even a rolled-up carpet balanced on their heads, roadside stalls, dust-covered trucks, and swarms of tricycle taxis, known here, as I'll find out later, by the Indian word *bajaj*. We pull into the forecourt of the Gondar Plaza Hotel. It's a modern 5-story building painted yellow and red and overlooking a bustling divided highway, with a pleasing band of greenery down the middle. We check in and I quickly discover how little English most people speak. It's an instant reminder of just how unique Ethiopia has always been, the lone country in Africa that apart Mussolini's six-year occupation successfully fought off European colonization.

At 4 pm it's time for our first meeting with "the Professor and the Fixer." I finally come face to face with Mulatu Wubneh, who I've known since June 2020 from the many engaging conversations we've had on Zoom and over the phone. In his mid-70s, Mulatu is still full of energy. His eyes sparkle behind his glasses as we shake hands. We've enjoyed our mutual interest in Gondar's wartime history. With him is Kebrom Tekle, a young man also wearing glasses and a frown of deep concentration. To put him at ease, I tell him, "Ah, so you're the fixer Mulatu has been raving about." On a previous stint as a visiting professor that was cut short by the Covid pandemic, Mulatu met and struck up a friendship with Kebrom. Impressed by his competence and calmness under pressure, he singled him out as the best candidate to pull off the unusual arrangements that my World War II explorations will require. Kebrom and I have been in touch by email for the last month laying the groundwork for my trip, including picking this hotel conveniently close to the university campus where Mulatu is living and teaching his classes.

It's time to start turning all my planning into reality. In the hotel lounge we find a quiet corner. I pull my father's artillery map out of its protective cylinder and unroll it on the table in front us. "Wow, you've had it enlarged," says Mulatu happily. Looking at a physical copy rather than a file on a computer screen brings home how remarkable this document truly is. As the legend says it was compiled and drawn from aerial photographs and ground reconnaissance. Somehow it was produced "in the field" 10 days before the attack on Gondar on Nov. 27, 1941. I point to the key locations I want to visit; Ayba Ridge where the 54th Nyasaland

Field Battery was positioned; its three primary battle targets which are the Italian forts or strongpoints on three ridges to the east of Gondar; and its fourth and most difficult target of all, the Italian battery which suddenly and unexpectedly began firing from a hill to the north of the city called Dunquam.

Each of these locations comes with its own particular logistical challenges, such as what kind of vehicle to use if the roads are rough. Or, if we have to go on foot, what kind of security risks could we face. Mulatu had already warned me that, even with the ceasefire with Tigray now in place, things aren't back to normal. People still remember the Tigrayan missiles striking close to the airport where we just landed. After talking with Kebrom, the two of them have come to the conclusion that we'll definitely need an armed guard to protect us in locations outside the city. The good news, says Kebrom, is that he's found a man who lives near where the 54th Nyasaland set up its guns who can probably serve as both guard and guide. But for starters so that we can get over jet lag and possibly altitude sickness — Gondar is close to 8,000 feet above sea level — he suggests we do something easy and close to home to start with. The obvious choice is Gondar's imperial castles which so enchanted the Italian occupiers that they quickly envisaged them becoming the centerpiece of a new provincial capital in their African empire. With that we wrap up our meeting. Scott and I are succumbing to jet lag. After an early dinner I have no trouble falling asleep. Shortly before dawn, though, I'm awakened by a dog that launches into a protracted barking spree. I've left the window open to take advantage of the breeze, forgetting that the room is on the front and therefore noisy side of the hotel. The dog's bark gives way to a human voice chanting. It's a mournful and insistent sound. Turning over and putting a pillow over my head, I make a mental note for the morning: "switch to a room in the back."

DAY TWO — Tuesday, 3/14/23

At 10am, Kebrom meets us in the hotel lobby. In his brown slacks, red shirt, and olive-green zip-up jacket, he's definitely more fashionably dressed than either Scott or me in our hiking gear. The three of us walk out onto the sidewalk in front of the hotel. The divided highway is already pulsing with traffic of all shapes and sizes, from big snarling Chinese-built trucks to buzzing Indian taxis, even the odd horse-drawn buggy. Kebrom explains that all the traffic is being diverted through here by construction work up on the main highway which runs behind the hotel. Another reason to switch to a room in the back. He yells "*Bajaj.*" The driver of one of the blue and white tricycle taxis pulls over. It's basically a modified motorbike which the driver controls with handlebars. The three of us cram into the hooded back seat and begin our first ride into the city center. With no side windows, sightseeing is limited. After following the divided highway for a mile or two, we make a sharp turn to the right. Kebrom tells us the rules for *bajaj* traffic force us to enter a warren of narrow streets that climb the hill on which the center of Gondar sits. Surprisingly some are paved with European-style cobblestones. But for a quasi-medieval city they seem very appropriate. On each side, makeshift shopping stalls cram any vacant space between as well as in front of the buildings.

Our first stop is a bank to change money, located in the heart of what was once the Italian part of town. After getting out of the *bajaj*, we climb an ornate flight of steps that bring us to a street where a pair of old Italian government buildings face each other, still painted their original shade of yellow. During the Italian occupation the street was known as Viale Re Imperatore, Avenue of the King Emperor. We turn left and walk along the stretch where mass rallies were once held. Our destination is the Commercial Bank's main branch. After trying in vain at several banks next to the hotel, I'm hugely relieved to find my American Express card works for cash withdrawals here.

The bank is only a few blocks from Fasil Ghebbi, as the main castle complex is called, so we set off on foot in that direction and soon encounter the first evidence of how World War II affected Gondar. We're walking alongside a steep embankment on top of which sits one of Gondar's most prominent churches. Near the base of the embankment and almost hidden behind a curtain of bushy green vegetation, Kebrom points out an old archway, now filled with stones. During the war, he tells us, it was used as an air raid shelter when British bombers began their attacks in 1941. The inhabitants may also have taken cover here six years earlier. The same Italians planes that Emperor Haile Selassie fired at with his anti-aircraft gun in Dessie had first dropped bombs near the imperial castles in Gondar setting fire to several grass huts below the walls with women and children still trapped inside.[19]

The road next to the embankment opens out into to Gondar's long central square, the place where the Italian quarter meets the Fasil Ghebbi castle complex. The north end of the square, where we are, is dominated by a golden statue of Gondar's hometown hero, Emperor Tewodros, father of modern Ethiopia. He stands defiantly with his sword and shield on top of a grey castle-like platform with a short, extremely wide-muzzled cannon mounted below him. I'll learn more about Tewodros later.

At the south end of the central square, I can see the crenellated battlements of one of Gondar's imperial castles looming above a 20-foot-high stone wall. Some tall trees rise above it too, their long branches casting some welcome shade over us as we follow the wall round to the entrance on the south side. Inside the main gate, Kebrom introduces us to Abebe Abiye, the guide he's lined up to give us the history of the place. Abebe, like Kebrom is in his late 20s, educated, knows his history, and has clearly been doing this for a while. He started off leading German groups, which meant of course mastering German, no mean achievement in itself. He leads us out from under the trees into an expanse of dry grass where I get my first real view of stone castles of Gondar. I'd seen pictures but they don't prepare you for the sheer size and variety of buildings. Inevitably the thought crosses my mind — did my father ever stand here? The complex covers 17 acres, Abebe tells us, surrounded by a half-mile long defensive wall pierced by 12 gates. 1,000 soldiers once

---

[19] Jeff Pierce, 'Prevail: The Inspiring Story of Ethiopia's Victory over Mussolini's Invasion' Ch. 10, p. 204.

stood guard over those gates. They give access to six castles built by six different emperors, as well as three churches.

British bombs may have caused destruction here too. Two stumps are all that's left of the main arch we pass through to reach the first and most imposing castle. It was built by Fasilides for whom the castle enclosure is named.[20] He became emperor in 1632 and within a few years founded the city of Gondar as his new permanent capital. Prior to that for almost two hundred years, the imperial court was an itinerant affair moving between different places. It feels as if I've entered a time warp, taking me back to a school history lesson about the medieval kings of England. Except I'm in Africa, and the names are exotically unfamiliar.

Fasilides it turns out picked Gondar for three very practical reasons — good climate, free of malaria, and good water supply from three rivers. And his timing was perfect. Gondar rapidly became an important trade hub with caravan routes going north through Sudan to Egypt and another heading east to the Red Sea. Gold, slaves, and coffee, which was becoming popular in Europe, were the main commodities traded. While Muslim merchants controlled the trade, the Gondaree ruling class shared in its profits. And these paid the masons and craftsmen who built the castles that followed. Within 70 years Gondar's population swelled to 70,000, a number it wouldn't reach again until the mid-20th century.

Fasilides' castle, also his palace, is the largest and most intact building inside the Castle Enclosure. Its Ethiopian features give it a magical and fantastic quality: round domes at the corners, balconies on two levels from which the emperor or his spokesman issued decrees, and a single tower rising in asymmetrical fashion near the southwest corner. Inside, the Star of David features prominently on one wall. It's the emblem of the Ethiopia's 3,000-year-old dynasty, stretching from Menelik I, son of Solomon and Sheba, all the way to Haile Selassie whose title, King of Judah, signified his descent from one of the twelve tribes of Israel. In the throne room, to protect himself from any would-be assassins, the emperor spoke to his officials and subjects through a window. Unfortunately, only the ground floor is accessible to visitors, so we have to imagine the chapel and other rooms that fill the space above. As we leave through the back door, we pass what looks

---

[20] Bahru Zewde, 'A History of modern Ethiopia, 1855-1991'(2001), p. 10.

like an empty swimming pool. In fact, it's a cistern that was used to collect rainwater for use in the long dry season which we're in now. Next to it stands a jacaranda tree covered in lilac flowers. Another reminder this is Africa not England. Although originally from South America, jacaranda trees lined the main street of Zomba, the town where I lived in Malawi as a child.

Abebe recommends we skip the second palace of Yohannes I. He levied no taxes on the people, perhaps explaining its modest size. Besides, the Italian restorers had also covered it in plaster to make it look more European when they transformed it into their military headquarters. Confusingly, the Gondar castles and palaces are often described as "Portuguese," particularly in wartime newsreels and older accounts. As Abebe goes on to explain, that's because the Portuguese were the first Europeans to arrive in Ethiopia in the 16th century. But traveling with those early explorers was an Indian mason named Abdal Kerim from the Portuguese colony of Goa. He brought with him the technique for making limestone mortar — a forerunner of cement — to better hold stones and therefore stone structures together.[21] The Ethiopians, having learned the technique, adapted it to create the style of architecture so majestically expressed in the Gondar palaces.

We move on to the palace of Yohannes' son, Iyasu I, also known as Iyasu the Great under whom the Ethiopian empire grew to its largest extent, encompassing all of the Horn of Africa. His palace is more of a ruin. Much of the roof is gone, apart from one room that has an unusual vaulted brick ceiling. It also has a curious anticlockwise spiral staircase because Iyasu was left-handed. The French explorer and physician, Charles-Jacques Poncet, who spent several years in Gondar and struck up a friendship with Iyasu, gave a glowing description of the emperor: "He is the most handsome man I have seen in Ethiopia. He is a lover of curious arts and sciences, but his chief passion is for war. He is brave and undaunted in battles, and always at the head of his troops."[22] Iyasu received the French explorer seated cross-legged on a couchlike throne covered in red damask with gold embroidery.

---

[21] Richard Pankhurst, 'History of Ethiopian Towns from the mid-19th century to 1935,' p. 107.

[22] Charles-Jacques Poncet, 'The Red Sea and Adjacent Countries at the close of the 17th Century,' edited by William Foster, The Hakluyt Society, 1949 pp. 130&116.

"He was bareheaded, and his hair braided very neatly. A great emerald glittered on his forehead." With Poncet's help, Iyasu built the most elaborate bath and sauna complex. It includes a deep subterranean chamber with no windows which Abebe leads us through inviting us to imagine it filled with steam. Adjoining it is a sanatorium. And nearby are the cages which housed the lions that symbolized Ethiopian imperial power. The last one lived there until as recently as 1981. Iyasu's long reign lasted until 1706. He had over 30 concubines which complicated the succession and ultimately weakened the Ethiopian monarchy.

The ruined theater hall Abebe leads us to next was built by one of Iyasu's sons, Emperor Dawit III, also known as Dawit the Singer. He was named after the biblical King David with whom he shared a love for music and song. Another reference to the tradition that links Ethiopian monarchs back to the Old Testament Jewish kings and the temple in Jerusalem. This time Abebe, attributes that link to *Kebra Nagast*, the national epic Scott had introduced me to in his Graham Hancock saga of the Ark.

The last palaces we visit at the north end of the complex are still reasonably well preserved. Emperor Bakaffa, another son of Iyasu, built a nine-horse stable and opposite it, his banquet hall. Abebe says the Scottish explorer, James Bruce — who in 1770 spent nearly two years in Gondar and the surrounding area in his quest for the source of the Nile — was invited to dine here but was appalled by what he called the Ethiopian tradition of eating raw meat "snatched from living animals." Bruce was a man of many talents. At 6ft 4 he was an expert horseman and marksman. At the same time, he was a scientist, scholar, linguist, and freemason. He left behind a voluminous account of his time in Ethiopia. In it he described Bakaffa as "silent, secret, and unfathomable in his designs, surrounded by soldiers who were his own slaves, and by new men of his own creation." From his own research into Bruce, Scott thinks he probably got his description of Bakaffa, from his wife, Empress Mentewab, whose daughter, Aster, Bruce struck up a friendship with and maybe something more, according to Abebe. Mentewab was a famously beautiful woman who the emperor had met while traveling in disguise through the province where she lived.[23] According to one story, when he fell ill,

---

[23] James Bruce 'Travels to Discover the Source of the Nile'(1790 edition), Vol. 2, Book 4, p. 599.

she nursed him back to health and as a reward he married her. When Bakaffa died she showed herself so adept at court politics that she ruled for more than 20 years as regent first to her son, Iyasu II and then her grandson, Iyoas. She built the last palace in the Fasil Ghebbi complex, an elegant two-story building with tall arched windows on each floor and topped with a crenellated tower and roof. It's the one I'd first seen looming above the outer wall as we walked across the Gondar's Italian-built main square.

Invading Italian forces led by none other than Achille Starace, secretary of the Italian Fascist Party and a fanatical supporter of Mussolini, occupied Gondar against little opposition on April 1st, 1936. By that time many of the castles we're seeing today were already in ruins or in need of repair. But to Italian eyes they seemed the Ethiopian equivalent of Rome's Colosseum and ancient Forum. Already the surrounding highlands they had traveled through reminded them, as historian Haile Larebo writes, of "a rolling countryside and salubrious climate likened to that of May in Italy."[24] Small wonder then, as Mulatu Wubneh had told me during one of our early phone conversations, that just months after the invasion, a well-known Italian architect named Gherardo Bosio, was hired to draw up a master plan turning Gondar into a *Secondo Roma*. As Mulatu put it in his definitive study of Gondar's urban history, "The Italian administration clearly saw the value of exploiting Gondar's long history and status as an imperial capital to enhance Italy's colonial power."[25]

Gondar was to become the capital of Amhara, one of the six regions that made up the new colony of Italian East Africa. Mussolini's grand vision called for several thousand Italians to make it their new home here. At same time, the city's master plan had to remain true to the Fascist doctrine of preventing interracial fraternization by creating separate neighborhoods. The castles therefore became both the center and dividing line between the races. The European quarter, primarily for

---

[24] Haile Larebo, 'The Building of an Empire: Italian Land Policy & Practice in Ethiopia, 1935-1941,' p. 143ani.

[25] Mulatu Wubneh, 'Urban resilience and sustainability of the city of Gondar (Ethiopia) in the face of adverse historical changes,' 'Planning Perspectives,' pp. 9-12.

https://www.tandfonline.com/doi/full/10.1080/02665433.2020.1753104

the upper class, would be built above the castles, while below them would be the indigenous quarter, clustered around the existing Qedame Gebeya, Saturday Market. Below that in Addis Alem there would also be a separate Muslim quarter and an Ethiopian Jewish quarter, Beth Israel, up in Wolleka to the north. To the west across the Qaha River there would be two additional European quarters for blue- and white-collar workers.

Two Cinecitta newsreels I'd found online from occupation period reveal how that plan was implemented and how the occupiers viewed Ethiopians. The first, produced in December 1936, eight months after the Italian occupation began, is titled "Gondar, ancient Ethiopian capital."[26] After the opening shots of the ruined castles it cuts to scenes of Ethiopian village life, including the preparation of *enjera* flat bread. On special occasions, villagers eat raw meat with gusto followed by dancing to frenetic drumbeats to aid the digestion. The final sequence moves back to the castles where, in a blatantly racist juxtaposition, shots of two monkeys grooming each other on a wall are intercut with an Ethiopian couple, similarly posed and touching each other with affection. The second newsreel, produced in January 1940, celebrates the visit of General Attile Teruzzi, minister for Africa. The opening images are of new buildings and flags on the Via Re Imperatore where I'd gone to change money. The opening montage shows a line of soldiers on motorbikes, a close up of two young white children and then ranks of settlers holding banners to greet the minister. Dressed in his general's uniform he waves from the balcony of Fasilides castle and then is seen walking beside Empress Mentewab's palace. From there, like us, he visits Gondar's main square with its newly completed telecommunications building and cinema, before getting a tour of a dam under construction, soon to be producing electricity. The newsreel celebrates the rapid progress of the Italian dream from which Ethiopians are either excluded or appear only as a distant faceless crowd.[27]

---

[26] Archivio Luce Cinecitta 'Gondar antica capitale etiopica' 12/02/1936 https://www.youtube.com/watch?v=RB4UvgvDuxY&list=PLDr7-T0J4QjEH7OSQdYnszte6Ipz0Og2C&index=287

[27] Archivio Luce Cinecitta 'Viista del Ministro Terruzi' 1/03/1940 https://www.youtube.com/watch?v=Mnnj2riq48o&list=PLDr7-T0J4QjEH7OSQdYnszte6Ipz0Og2C&index=286

By the time our guide Abebe's introduction to Gondar's golden age comes to an end back in front of Fasilides castle, he's given us a clear and often colorful picture of the personalities and political rivalries which gave rise to the creation of these majestic buildings. And also, how the Italian occupiers gleefully appropriated them as part of their colonial vision. It seems like a good time to break for lunch but only, as we quickly discover, for Scott and I. Kebrom and Abebe won't be joining us. Since it's Lent, like most of Ethiopia's practicing Christians, they must wait until 3pm to break their fast. As we leave through the main gate where the *bajaj* taxis congregate looking for fares, Abebe points out one more crucial and very much living piece of history. In the center of a traffic circle, its branches spreading out and covering the entire space, stands a giant sycamore tree. It's called *Jan Tekel* which means King's Tree, Abebe tells us. Legend has it this is where Emperor Fasilides first pitched his tent when he decided to make Gondar his capital nearly four centuries ago.

In late afternoon the four of us resume our journey through early Gondar history. It starts with another cramped and bumpy *bajaj* ride this time to the Fasilides baths about a mile and half to the west of the main castle complex. This is where either the emperor or his grandson, Iyasu, built a smaller palace in what was once a lush green forest. As Abebe tells us, the spot was chosen because of its proximity to the Qaha River. Part of the river was diverted through an underground channel to fill what looks like a giant swimming pool. At one end, mounted on stone columns stands a small two-story palace reachable by a single bridge spanning the water. At the far end of the pool a second channel returns the water to the main river. In historic times the basin was kept full year-round but now it's only filled during Timkat, the Ethiopian Epiphany, when as many as 10,000 visitors gather inside the palace grounds to celebrate Christ's baptism by John the Baptist. At the culmination of the 3-day ceremony, the bishop and clergy bless the waters, which is the signal for young boys and girls to jump in and revel in them.

Incredibly, it's already been three years since I visited the Ethiopian Community Association in Atlanta where I first learned about the importance of the Timkat festival for Gondar. Now here I am standing on the very site where it's celebrated. When the pool is empty, as it is now, the most remarkable sight, besides the palace itself, are the huge banyan and fig trees whose yellow, sinewy limbs grasp the surrounding walls in a flesh-like embrace. The emperor also picked this site because it offers a rare piece of level ground in Gondar's otherwise hilly terrain. A place where the nobility could practice the arts of war — horse riding and shooting. In one corner a favorite royal horse named Zobel was buried in an ornate mausoleum.

The last leg of our Gondar history tour requires one more *bajaj* ride up a hill not far from the Fasilides bath. This is the one I most eager to see because of a possible connection to my father's World War II experience. At our meeting yesterday, Mulatu said he believes it could be where the 54th Nyasaland Field Battery were aiming as they tried to destroy their most distant target, north of Gondar. On the artillery map it's called Dunquam, perhaps a misreading of the similar-sounding Qusquam. The *bajaj* begins climbing a steep incline passing a group of busy market stalls. A little further up a group of thatched conical huts are perched on the hillside. These house monastic students, Kebrom informs us, 10-to-12-year-old kids who have come here for several weeks of bible study. Then we arrive at Qusquam, the name of both the church and the adjacent palace built by Empress Mentewab, the famously beautiful wife of Bakaffa we heard about this morning and whose daughter, Aster, the Scottish explorer, James Bruce, was so taken with.

The church, like most in Ethiopia, is circular. It's a modern restoration, built by Haile Selassie. The original one was destroyed by the Sudanese Mahdi whose army sacked Gondar in 1888.[28] It was led by the successor to the original Mahdi, famous for destroying a British army under General Gordon of Khartoum. The Mahdists then attacked Ethiopia, which had become an ally of the British. The church has a green corrugated iron roof with an eight-pointed star at its peak. The earliest churches were caves, says Abebe. Then they became rectangular or square. And from the 16th century on they became round. The surrounding stone wall is original. Its eight domed towers were once inhabited by hermits who spent much of their time here in prayer. Also forming part of the wall is a larger square structure in which the "Abune" or Patriarch lived. As we're looking at his residence and the grove of indigenous juniper trees that surrounds it, a priest in a white turban arrives with a set of keys. The first unlocks a gate in the wall leading to the palace beyond

---

[28] Bahru Zewde, 'A History of Modern Ethiopia, 1855-1991 (2001).

but more intriguingly the second key lets us into a museum housed in the basement of the Abune's tower home. This cramped space contains a surprising collection of ancient artifacts - a large drum, beating it was the traditional way news was transmitted, along with several old, illuminated books and paintings. Most astonishing of all, in one corner lies a small wooden casket with a glass panel in its lid. Through it we can see several partial skeletons, said to belong to Empress Mentewab, her son and grandson.

Back outside we find ourselves standing in front of the ruins of Mentewab's Palace. This, Abebe tells us, is where the empress retreated and lived with her daughters in mourning for the death of her grandson, whose skeletal remains we'd just seen in the casket with her. From his own studies, Scott adds that James Bruce was summoned here soon after he arrived in Gondar for one specific purpose. There was an outbreak of smallpox at the time he arrived and because he knew how to successfully treat the disease, he was brought to Qusquam palace at the request of Mentewab's daughter, Aster.[29] Several of her younger family members were suffering from the disease. They were being kept in darkened, musty rooms filled with pictures of healing saints. But that traditional remedy wasn't working. Bruce's prescription was to open all the windows to allow in fresh air, fumigate the rooms with incense and wash the victims in warm water. Within a few days all but one of them started to recover. According to Abebe, Aster was profoundly grateful to Bruce, even going so far as to turn on her sexual charms. But more crucially she also did him a huge political favor. She sent word of Bruce's healing accomplishment, which included their own youngest son, to her husband, Ras Mikael Sehul. He was a prince from the neighboring province of Tigray who had become the real powerbroker in Gondar at the time and someone who Bruce was desperately trying to get an audience with.

Then comes a real bombshell, literally. Abebe tells us that large sections of the palace were destroyed by British artillery fire in World War II. Immediately the thought flashes through my mind — if this is Dunquam Hill, as Mulatu contends, then some of the shells that Sgt. Bruce Wickham's unit fired at the Italian guns

---

[29] James Bruce, 'Travels to Discover the Source of the Nile'(1790 edition) Vol. 3 Book 5, Ch. 8, pp. 209-215.

positioned nearby must have missed their mark, destroying instead James Bruce's one time bedroom and other parts of this 300-year-old palace!

Reveling in the strong reaction he just inspired, Abebe decides to follow this revelation with a more bawdy tale. The most famous room in Mentewab's palace was the banquet hall which remains largely intact with exquisite carvings of an elephant and a lion on its facade. One day, some of her courtiers begged her to throw them a party here. To their surprise and delight, she agreed but on one condition, one deviously calculated to demonstrate her absolute power over them: during the festivities they couldn't go to the bathroom to relieve themselves. After a few hours of celebrating some guests began to fidget uncomfortably. Then one innocently asked the empress a question, "What is 500 plus 500?" The answer in Amharic is *Shinawa*, meaning 1,000 which Mentewab duly gave. But it also sounds something like a phrase meaning "Please relieve yourselves." Immediately there was a mad scramble for the nearest toilet. The guests had got the last laugh.

Leaving behind Qusquam palace and church, we walk further up the hill. If Qusquam really is Dunquam as Mulatu contends and which Abebe's story of British shelling seems to confirm, then I need to find a vantage point up higher, above the trees surrounding Qusqam. From there I should be able to see a crucial landmark — Ayba Ridge, off to the east, where the 54th Nyasaland was positioned for the assault on Gondar. I'd studied that ridge enough on Google Earth to know its features and using the Artillery Map had calculated the distances closely enough to identify where the guns were most likely positioned. It's a high point in the shape of a pyramid but with the top lopped off.

As we scramble up a slope to the outskirts of a village a young girl in a bright red blouse and pink dress standing next to one of nearest buildings studies us carefully. At the top of the slope I turn and look. In a break between a row of eucalyptus trees I catch my first glimpse of Ayba Ridge now bathed in late afternoon sunshine. I pull out my father's old binoculars I've brought with me — not the ones he had with him in 1941, but still appropriate for this moment. I focus on the ridge, move a bit to the right and there is the truncated pyramid I'm looking for. Elated, I point it out to Scott and Kebrom. Not in my wildest dreams did I expect to make a major discovery so early on in the trip. And here I am making two already — my father's battery position, nine miles away, and right below us at the very edge of their guns' range, their most difficult target, Dunquam Hill!

DAY THREE — Wednesday, 3/15/23

Yesterday's discoveries at Qusquam felt like pure gifts and blind luck. Today is the day when I imagined my Gondar World War II expedition might first produce tangible results. Kebrom hails our now familiar mode of transportation, a *bajaj*. We even follow the same route through town to reach one of the highest points in its northeast corner. On a hill in the shade of a thick tree-canopy sits Gondar's most famous church — Debre Birhan Selassie. We meet up with our guide Abebe Abiye again. Today he's dressed relaxed casual, blue jeans, check shirt over yellow tee. He begins to tell the church's story. The name means "Trinity on the Mount of Light." Although it was built in 1679 by Emperor Iyasu the Great, its rectangular form deliberately harks back to a much earlier period — the shape of churches built in the 4th century in Ethiopia's first capital, Axum. It was intended to be the new home of the Ark of the Covenant also housed in Axum. But a storm mysteriously prevented the transfer so a replica of the Ark as well as the name was brought from the town of Debre Birhan. What makes Debre Birhan Selassie the most famous church in Gondar is that it alone among Gondar's churches survived the Muslim Mahdists' sacking in 1888.[30] Legend has it that it was saved by a swarm of bees that flew down and drove off the Mahdi's soldiers carrying flaming torches to set it on fire.

We remove our shoes and for the first time I enter an Ethiopian Church. The four walls and ceiling are covered in brightly colored murals painted over 350 years ago. Some scenes are familiar; others have a distinctly Ethiopian flavor. The portrait of Mary above the front door shows her wearing a blue dress in the shape of the map of Ethiopia. There's St. George slaying the dragon often seen as a metaphor for Emperor Menelik II triumphing over an Italian army at Adowa in 1896, an earlier ignominious Italian defeat that Mussolini sought to avenge. The ceiling is adorned with the heads of angels with distinctly Ethiopian features. The most

---

[30] Bahru Zewde, *A History of Modern Ethiopia, 1855-1991 (2001)*, p. 59.

controversial image shows Satan leading the prophet Mohammed on a camel. One reason the Islamic Mahdists would have wanted to destroy it. The whole church complex is a mass of symbols. The perfectly round outer wall symbolizes the world. It has 12 towers, one for each of the apostles, the 13th, the front gate built in shape of a lion with a section of the curving wall as its tail, represents Jesus. The rectangular shape of the church itself recalls Noah's Ark.

Fascinating as it is, religion is not what drew me here. Debre Birhan church happens to be the only landmark common to both my father's artillery map and Google Maps and Google Earth, the modern references I used to plan my search. As the crow flies the church is just over 6 miles west of where his battery was dug in on Ayba Ridge — by the lopped-off pyramid I saw for the first time yesterday. The page from the War Diary listing the targets for the 54th Nyasaland even describes one of them as "the track leading to Debre Birhan." It was the main supply route to the Italian strongpoint on top of the high ridge immediately to the east of the church. In the War Diary it's called *Deflecha* but locals know it as "Defecha." That's where we'll be heading shortly in the only way possible — on foot.

Before we set off, Abebe delivers one final surprise. Knowing the focus of my search, he's been asking around. He introduces me to an older man dressed smartly in a blue suit and cap named Feleke Sinke Ayalew who works as a church gatekeeper. He just told him an interesting story from World War II. His father was a resistance fighter with the local Ethiopian Patriot forces during the battle of Gondar. According to him, a British shell struck part of the stone wall surrounding the church. The scar, he says, is still visible. Quickly we make our way round to that part of the wall which does indeed face east where the British guns were positioned. Scanning its upper section, I make out a blackened patch spreading across several shattered stones. The damage seems too minimal to be caused by one of the 25-pound explosive shells my father's unit were firing. Especially since, as we saw yesterday, the same guns appeared to have destroyed massive chunks of the walls at Qusquam palace. But the War Diary records a second Indian artillery unit, the 22nd Mountain Battery, also taking part in the attack. They were using smaller guns that fired much lighter and less destructive shells. Conceivably one of these could have caused the damage to the outer wall. In any case Feleke in his blue suit and I have something precious in common — both our fathers helped liberate Gondar. We stand together while Kebrom takes our photo.

When we return to the front gate of Debre Birhan church, I come face to face with another startling echo of World War II. Two men in camouflage and armed with Kalashnikov AK-47 rifles are standing waiting for us. Kebrom has hired them to be our guards on the hike to Defecha Ridge. When he started making inquiries about who could provide protection in the more remote places my search would take us, one of his contacts put him in touch with two off-duty members of Gondar's own city militia, popularly known as Peacekeepers. They're a stark reminder that just a few months ago Ethiopia was engaged in another brutal war. Only in November 2022 did the Federal Government in Addis Ababa sign a ceasefire agreement with the province of Tigray after two years of conflict in which over half a million people lost their lives. These two men, Alemu and Yohannes, are part of the force that Gondar employed to step up security during that time against a possible Tigrayan incursion. Besides protection, Kebrom says they can provide another important benefit. Because of their work they know the countryside around Gondar like the back of their hand and can guide us where need to go.

At 11:30am, Alemu, the older of the two guards, sets us off at a brisk pace, heading down the hill behind Debre Birhan church towards Defecha Ridge. Yohannes, whose uniform is newer and carries himself more formally, brings up the rear. We pass through a collection of houses in a grove of eucalyptus trees, a high point where the Italian military once had their main observation post, before zig-zagging down a much steeper incline. Instead of turning south as I expect, Alemu is heading more to the north. That's odd. But then I remember that we have to cross the Angereb River that runs through this valley. From Google Earth I know there's been one major change since World War II — the river's been dammed, and the dam wall will be the easiest place to cross. Sure enough, we're soon walking along the well-worn path along the top of it, ready to begin our ascent up Defecha Ridge on top of which the Italian forces had built a key defensive position.

It's a hard climb, especially as Alemu, with his AK-47 now slung across his shoulders, is tending to favor the shortest route; virtually straight up over rocks — some of them loose so you have to constantly watch your step — and through the parched yellow scrub. The dryness of the air is already affecting my sinuses. On top of that we're at 8,000 feet and hardly truly acclimated to the altitude yet.

As well as long distance running, Ethiopians clearly have walking in their bones. Kebrom doesn't claim to take any regular exercise but he's easily keeping up with Alemu ahead of me. On top of which, as I now know, they're fasting for Lent which means no food and no water even until later in the day. I'm glad I'm a runner myself otherwise I doubt I'd be in good enough shape to climb at this pace. Thankfully Scott is a seasoned hiker too, a skill he's honed in exotic places like Tibet.

After half an hour we crest the ridge and start walking along a path through dark, recently ploughed fields. Our first objective is another church, this one named Defecha Kidanemihret, "Covenant of Mercy." As we approach, we hear chanting. Through a screen of trees we can make out a crowd of people gathered in a field below the church. Alemu stops beside a stone wall a priest is preparing to climb over. He's wearing a bright orange cape elaborately embroidered with gold symbols and holding aloft a large multi-colored umbrella fringed with white tassels to shade him from the sun. Once he's over the wall, a maneuver he manages with the ease born of practice, Alemu approaches him, and the priest immediately offers him his double-headed silver cross. Alemu touches his forehead to it and then each of his cheeks, bowing as he retreats to let the priest pass. This from a man carrying a rifle on his shoulder.

Following the priest, we continue past what look like a pair of barns with a donkey tethered next to them and on through a green wooden gate leading to the church. Originally it was built by Bakaffa, Kebrom tell us, one of Gondar's emperors whose banquet hall we saw yesterday, but recently it's been modernized. Its pink iron roof is fringed with red, green and yellow, the Ethiopian colors. We peer through an open door where people are entering but Kebrom signals that we shouldn't follow. To show our respect he makes a small donation and then we turn to move on. At the time the biggest impressions this church made on me were its age and inner mystery. But later it would play a more practical, even pivotal role in my search for my father's World War II sites.

Our route towards the southern end of Defecha Ridge now takes us past the crowd we'd glimpsed and heard earlier. They're here for a funeral, a hundred or more people dressed mainly in white gathered in a field behind a low stone wall to pay their respects. I ask Kebrom if the large crowd means someone important has died. Quietly he replies "no, they do that for everyone." As we skirt the burial ceremony, I catch sight of a group of priests holding up their bright umbrellas and the colorful fabrics draped over the coffin in their midst. They lighten an otherwise somber ceremony.

Leaving behind this brief but vivid glimpse into the life of this village makes me wonder how much has really changed in the 80 years that separate us from World War II. Probably the church and small farms looked much the same except back then many this close to Gondar may have been deserted. The British War Diaries speak off encountering refugees fleeing the conflict zone.

In contrast, when I look round after a few minutes of renewed hiking I see a crowd of curious children following us, clearly intrigued by what this strange group of five men — two white and two with guns — are up to in their part of the countryside. Perhaps they've come from the funeral or may be school's over for the day. They continue walking with us, fixing us with a quiet but curious stare.

We come to a fork in the path. Alemu seems ready to veer right on a path heading downhill. I ask Kebrom why? He consults with Alemu — it's the way to Maldiba Ridge, our next destination. But from studying Google Earth I know that we haven't even reached the key part of Defecha Ridge yet. The 54th Nyasaland's most important initial target was an Italian strongpoint at the South end, said to be located in "an old Portuguese fort." After more consultation, Kebrom says Alemu knew of what he calls a "bastion" and we take the left fork instead. That keeps us on the ridge crest and intuitively feels better. As if confirming my hunch, Alemu soon stops up ahead. There's a break in the brush growing behind the stone wall on the eastern side of our path. He points to a lone bald peak and says emphatically, "Ganz." Gantz Hill, I knew from the War Diary, was where 54th Nyasaland's Forward Observation officer and his assistant were posted to help direct fire.[31] It's also marked on the artillery map. And beyond Gantz and slightly to the left I can see looming the brown hulk of Ayba Ridge where the 54th were positioned. Another indication we're headed in the right direction.

Hiking on, a detail from another of the War Diaries keeps coming into my mind. It was from 2/2 KAR, the Nyasaland infantry battalion, also newly formed and unbattle-tested like my father's artillery unit. Their objective was to climb

---

[31] War Diary of 54th Nyasaland Field Battery Nov. 27, 1941, (See Appendix).

Defecha Ridge via one of two "re-entrants" at the south end.[32] Re-entrant is a topographical term for a gulley running down a slope. But we're walking too near the center of the ridge to be able see its downhill slope. I see a path going at right angles to ours and instinctively feel we should follow it. Yohannes, our second younger guard who usually defers to Alemu, agrees. The going is rougher, full of large mud-covered rocks. After a quarter of a mile, we break through the waist-high vegetation and come out into an open area. After a few more steps the slope of Defecha Ridge descending into the valley beyond comes into view. To my left the land curves back behind us. Definitely a re-entrant.

The slope in front of me is steep, steeper than the one we had to climb up from the Angereb dam. Like Ethiopians, the Nyasaland infantry soldiers of 2/2 KAR, were used to moving through hilly terrain. But these men had more than just a steep slope to contend with on the morning of Nov. 27, 1941. As they tried to scramble up Defecha, they ran into a minefield and boobytraps. At the same time, they came under fire from Italian machine guns and artillery from the strongpoint on the top of the ridge. In the first two hours they struggled to make progress and were taking heavy casualties.[33] Fortunately, the observation officer with the second artillery unit, the 22nd Indian Mountain Battery, was close enough to see what was happening. Around 10:45 he radioed the 54th Nyasaland urgently calling for "rapid-fire" artillery support. Around the same time, the Gantz Hill observers, who had finally managed to establish radio contact after being jammed by the enemy, frantically called in the same request. All eight of the battery's guns immediately opened fire. It was Sgt. Bruce Wickham and the 54th Nyasaland's first real test. In just six minutes they managed to fire off 76 high explosive shells which slammed into the south end of Defecha Ridge, six miles away and close to where we're now standing.[34]

Kebrom relays this story to Alemu, our guard and lead guide. He peers intently down at the landscape, as if like me, he's imagining this 80-year old battle unfolding in front of us. As Kebrom finishes, he gestures to me: "And Jonathan's father

---

[32] War Diary of 26th Infantry Brigade Appendix B to Op. Order 28 Artillery Support Fire UK National Archives WO 169/2918

[33] Lt. Col. Hubert Moyse-Bartlett, 'The King's African Rifles,' Vol. 2, Ch. 21, pp.152/565.

[34] War Diary of 54th Nyasaland Field Battery Nov. 27, 1941, (See Appendix).

was one of those firing the guns." Alemu's looks me in the eye, his intense expression has now softened to a smile. He crosses one arm across his chest. "Your father fought alongside our fathers that day," he says. Something about this short, wiry man, perhaps it's the deep lines under his eyes, tells me he is no stranger to the horrors of war.

As we make our way back to the main path, two loaded donkeys suddenly appear in front of us, apparently knowing their way without any human to guide them. Only when we come round the next bend do we see their owner, a woman in her working clothes. She passes us without a glance, as if we're moving in a parallel universe. And in sense we are. I'm still thinking of the 2/2 KAR soldiers that day trying to climb up the murderous slope of Defecha through detonating mines, bursting shells and a hail of Italian machine-gun fire. Out of a company of 200 men, 18 were killed and 96 wounded.[35] I remember as a child visiting the tall brick war memorial outside Zomba, the old capital of Malawi, surrounded by red-flowering flamboyant trees. I hoped their names were inscribed somewhere on its walls.

We continue on towards the South end of Defecha Ridge. The path has almost vanished, and the vegetation has become thicker and wilder. In defiance of the lack of rain, purple flowers are blooming in profusion all around us. Then Alemu points out the "bastion." I see a rock wall almost hidden amongst the brush and trees. Was this really the old Portuguese fort, the Italian strong point whose guns were wreaking havoc among the men of the 2/2 KAR infantry? It seems so unimpressive. Evidently Alemu thought so too. Or maybe the images of battle it conjures up are all too vivid, jarring loose painful memories of his own he'd rather forget. After barely a pause, he moves on.

We pass a farm whose details make me think I'd really stepped into an 80-year time warp. Three round stacks of hay, made from straw so short it had clearly been threshed by circling oxen; a cow lying on the ground slowly chewing in the afternoon heat; a chicken scratching for something to eat nearby. Then a young boy appears from behind a tree and watches us go by.

---

[35] Lt. Col. Hubert Moyse-Bartlett, 'The King's African Rifles' Vol. 2, Ch. 21, p. 152/565.

Alemu leads us round a stand of trees and starts to climb what looks like the final hill of Defecha. As steep as it is, a farmer has somehow managed to plow it. I can see a dark silhouette that looks like a wall along the summit. As I scramble to the top, I see black stone steps leading down into what is clearly a fortified enclosure. Alemu steps down into it and obliges by taking up position as if about to fire his rifle over the parapet. Climbing down the other side and looking back I can see that, Portuguese or otherwise, this definitely constitutes a fort made of jet-black stone. Then Alemu through Kebrom informs us that this is Maldiba, the second Italian fortified ridge that the British were to attack once Defecha had fallen. I'm baffled. Was I missing something? Had we somehow crossed the low point between the two ridges?

By now we'd been hiking for more than two hours. Over a loudspeaker, the sound of chanting begins to rise from a church or community below. I suddenly realize that it's similar to the pre-dawn chant I heard during my first night in the hotel. But this time it has a more hopeful, buoyant sound. It's the signal, Kebrom tells us, that the day's Lenten fast is coming to a close. Alemu, anxious to get to food and water I'm sure, sets off at a cracking pace downhill through a eucalyptus grove and then through more newly plowed fields on the back side of whatever ridge we're on.

Soon the fields flatten out and beyond the corrugated-iron roofs of farmhouses I see a river threading its way through a rocky gorge ahead. This must be the Angereb emerging below the dam we'd crossed hours ago. Then an improbably ancient sight appears in front of me, although since this is Ethiopia, the country with a three-thousand-year history, things are seldom improbably ancient. A stone bridge with a single remaining entrance arch at one end spans the river and takes us across. Kebrom informs me it was built by Fasilides, the same emperor who built the first castle in Gondar.

Back at the hotel after some food and rest, I return to the puzzle of the final rock fort we had seen. Hoping the power doesn't go out — a frequent early evening occurrence I'm discovering here in Gondar — I pull up Google Earth and revisit our route that began at Debre Birhan church. On top of the Defecha Ridge I recognize the round pink roof of Defecha Kidanemihret church where the funeral ceremony was in progress. There's the steep slope with its minefield where the 2/2 KAR infantry attack had faltered and the 54th Nyasaland had helped them out with 76 rapidly fired shells. Moving on towards the south end I come to an open field with a fringe of forest that plunges down to a village below. And as I zoom in on the field above the forest I can clearly make out a square edged with black. It perfectly matches the Defecha fort location marked on the 54th Nyasaland's artillery map. According to the War Diary, they clearly hit their mark. The final entry reads "Enemy abandoned entire position setting fire to ammunition dump." In their first major action my father and his African gun crew had shown their worth. With the bare minimum of training on a brand-new weapon they'd still managed to hit their target when it counted. Sitting back in amazement in front of my computer screen, a thought crosses my mind: in just two days I've already found two of the targets assigned to my father and the 54th Nyasaland Field Battery on Nov. 27, 1941. And perhaps I'm the first person in 80 years to visit them and recognize their significance.

DAY FOUR — Thursday, 3/16/23

The most important objective of my Gondar World War II trip is to find the spot where the 54th Nyasaland were positioned on the day of the assault on Gondar. Originally, Kebrom had lined up a local man from the nearby village of Ayba — written as "Aiva" on the artillery map — who seemed perfect for the job both as our guard and guide. He had family memories of World War II that he promised to share. But when it came to negotiating a fee, he suddenly announced he wanted $450, nine times the going rate. Kebrom said the man admitted he was short of money and needed a big pay out. So, with Kebrom still working the problem of finding his replacement we decide to take a break from the city and go south to Gorgora for the day. It's the place where the campaign to retake Gondar got started, led by one of Ethiopia's few but very effective regular forces.

This time we're traveling in the comfort of a real car, a Toyota Corolla. Private cars are rare in Gondar. But only minutes into the trip, the traffic on the main divided highway grinds to a sudden halt. We inch forward for a while but then Teddy, our driver, and Kebrom decide it isn't going to get better any time soon. We follow in the wake of a minibus squeezing its way towards the right shoulder, presumably looking for an exit, I think. But then the minibus makes a 90-degree turn somehow nosing its way across the stalled traffic. We follow. Without any help from traffic police or other authorities, the outside lane, by mutual and mysterious agreement between drivers, is turned into a route heading back towards the city. Within minutes we find an alternative route and are once again heading towards our original destination.

Gorgora is about 60 kilometers south of Gondar. It's on the north shore of Lake Tana, fabled source of the Blue Nile or *Abay* as the Ethiopians call it. Incredibly, this branch of the world's longest river provides over 80 percent of its water flow during the rainy season as well as much of the rich silt that the Egypt's agriculture, and much of its economy in general, depends on. By World War II and even well before the British had for this reason seized effective control of Egypt and Sudan, its neighbor to the south where the Blue and White Niles meet. Egypt at the same time, controlled access to a second waterway vital to British trade and military interests, the Suez Canal. Small wonder then that after the capture of Gondar on April 1st, 1936, Mussolini immediately ordered his commander, Achille Starace, to continue south. If Italy controlled the Blue Nile, Mussolini believed, it would be well positioned at some point in the future to shift the balance of power still further in its favor.

Within two days, as the culmination of what Starace boasted was "the most risky, most difficult and most important venture" of the entire Italian campaign, his mobile column seized Gorgora, establishing a garrison there to control the lake and be ready to prevent any British incursion from Sudan to the west. Starace, who also served as secretary of the Italian Fascist Party, would eventually suffer the same fate as Mussolini. Both were executed by anti-fascist Italian partisans in April 1945 and their bodies strung up for all to see on one of the main streets in Milan.

In early November 1941, the campaign to free Gondar by British forces and Ethiopian Patriots was launched from the north shore of Lake Tana.[36] It was led by 2nd Ethiopian Battalion, a battle-hardened group of 350 men, Ethiopian exiles for the most part with a handful of British officers. They had originally formed part of Wingate's Gideon Force which had fought its way into the Ethiopian interior from Sudan. In May 1941 they had proudly marched into Addis Ababa ahead of Emperor Haile Selassie as he made his triumphal return. Now the 2nd Ethiopian Battalion was marching along the same road we're traveling, tasked with seizing Gianda, the first Italian strong point barring the way to Gondar itself with a garrison of 120 men.

The battle began a little before dawn on November 11. After quickly breaking through the Italian garrison's outer defenses, the battalion's advance was stopped by deadly machine-gun fire from a heavily fortified 2-story blockhouse in the center of Gianda. Suffering heavy casualties, including two veteran officers killed, one Ethiopian and one British, the battalion commander Colonel Benson was about to call a retreat. At that moment the tables turned. A British officer known for his

---

[36] David Shirreff, 'Bare Feet and Bandoliers: Wingate, Sandford, the Patriots and the Liberation of Ethiopia,' 2009, p. 251-253.

strong throwing arm managed to lob two grenades into the verandah of the blockhouse. While a sergeant set fire to the building next-door through ingeniously combining a Verey pistol with a cigarette lighter. Overhead a lone British fighter plane appeared, raking the blockhouse with machine-gun fire. At 9:45am the Ethiopian officer, Captain Werku Destu led the decisive charge, "hurling hand grenades and killing many of enemy." When the Italian commander surrendered, Werku hoisted the Ethiopian flag above the blockhouse. With that the 2nd Ethiopian Battalion had achieved its objective. From there it would go on to keep the much larger Italian garrison down in Gorgora bottled up and isolated until Gondar itself was taken.

This opening clash of the Gondar campaign always intrigued me. It took place on the very same day that Major Bingham, the commander of my father's artillery unit, the 54th Nyasaland, received word that *The City of Paris*, the cargo ship carrying the 25-pounder guns he and his men desperately needed, was about to dock in the Red Sea port of Massawa. After seeing how many Italian buildings had survived in Gondar it seemed there was a good chance the two-story blockhouse that figured so prominently in Gianda battle would still be standing. So, about half an hour into the drive we stop to get directions to Gianda or Genda as the locals call it. Kebrom's follow-up question about whether the blockhouse is still there initially draws just blank looks. But then, a man sporting a Bob Marley t-shirt steps forward. Yes, he says, the building is still standing but we've already passed the turn several miles back. Rather than turn around now we decide to catch it on the return journey.

Soon we enter the outskirts of Gorgora. Kebrom points to a hill to our right. On the top stands a towering stone column. "Shall we drive up there?" Immediately I recognize it as Mussolini's monument to his conquest of Ethiopia. "No, I don't think so. I've already seen it," I reply. Kebrom looks puzzled, so I explain, "I saw it in an old Italian newsreel. That was enough."

During my research I'd come across the film dated July 1938. It shows General Attile Teruzzi, the minister for Italian East Africa who would later salute the settlers in Gondar and tour its new buildings, arriving by plane on his first visit to Ethiopia. He had come to preside over the monument's dedication ceremony. Surrounded by Blackshirts, members of the Fascist militia who formed part of

Starace's invasion force that took Gondar and then Lake Tana, he salutes to a white crowd of military and civilians.[37]

I'd also found some contemporary photos showing the monument as it looks now, cracked but still standing. It's shaped like an axe wrapped in a bundle of staves, the Fascist power symbol. On one side is carved an Ethiopian lion, mortally wounded by a sword, while on the other a she-wolf suckles Romulus and Remus above the inscription "Rome Rules."

In the newsreel, after General Terruzi's dedication, a priest gives a blessing, sprinkling holy water at the foot of the monument. Then a plane is seen flying overhead to inaugurate the monument's second, more practical purpose. It was to serve as a lighthouse, with a beam mounted at the top that could shine across Lake Tana. The final scenes show a conductor leading a military band in a rousing tune as an all-white crowd of spectators watches the launch of several motorboats. Their job would be to control all traffic and commerce on the new Italian imperial lake.

As we continue along the road to Gorgora we suddenly find the way ahead is blocked. A guard tells us it's due to construction. A big new tourist eco-lodge, heavily promoted by the Federal Government, is being built on the shores of Lake Tana. Prime Minister Abiy Ahmed himself has even talked up its timeshare condos as a way to entice investors among the Ethiopian diaspora.[38] We circle back and make our way into town by another route. The road ends above a rocky beach leading down to the blue waters of Lake Tana. Here all signs of the Italian occupation, the long wooden jetty shown in the newsreel next to where the boats were launched as well as the buildings that housed a garrison of 1,500 men, seem to have disappeared.

The most prominent structure we find is one that is centuries older than anything the Italians built — Debresina Mariam church. Its curved wooden walls and

---

[37] Archivio Luce Cinecitta 'La Visita de Terruzi' 13/07/1938 https://www.youtube.com/watch?v=G5lW9Vhu4z4&list=PLDr7-T0J4QjEH7OSQdYnszte6Ipz0Og2C&index=354

[38] Further Africa, 'Ethiopia invites diaspora to invest in Gorgora Ecolodge' Jan. 19, 2022

https://furtherafrica.com/2022/01/19/ethiopia-invites-diaspora-to-invest-in-gorgora-ecolodge/

thatched roof are older even than any we've seen in Gondar. It was built in the late 16th century by Emperor Susenyos, father of Fasilides, Gondar's founder. It serves a monastery that's older still, founded in the 14th century. We're met by the abbot in his bright saffron robes and maroon cap. But our real guide is to be Endeshew, a bald man in a striped shirt and jeans who carries a priest's staff topped with brass ram's horns.

Unlike the church we saw yesterday up on Defecha Ridge, Gorgora is a regular tourist destination. This time after removing our shoes we're invited to enter through the main door, still made of the original wood. The church roof is supported by 12 wooden columns, one for each of the apostles. Endeshew dramatically pulls back a curtain and with his priest's staff points to what he calls the earliest Gondar-style painting of St. George slaying the dragon. The four walls of the inner sanctuary are covered with murals, but being a century older, their colors are more faded than those we saw yesterday at Debre Birhan church. An image of St. Raphael covers the door to the inner sanctuary, painted in what Endeshew calls "Indian-style." Standing with his sword dramatically raised he does look like a Hindu god, ready to strike any evildoers attempting to enter and steal the sacred tabots within. These replicas of the tablets on which the ten commandments are inscribed are held in every Ethiopian church. Elsewhere the evildoers themselves are actually portrayed, always one-eyed to make them easily recognizable — the brown devils of hell greeting unfortunate sinners; King Herod receiving the head of John the Baptist, freshly severed. These as well as the many uplifting images of the saints and of the Virgin Mary watch over the monks who pray here for 24 hours every Saturday. 20 of them live at the monastery, the abbot informs us, as we leave. The youngest is 23 and the oldest claims to be a remarkable 137 years old!

Back out in the daylight we head once again towards the shore of Lake Tana. It's already clear that any traces of the Italian occupation apart from Mussolini's monument perched on its high hill have long since disappeared. Or else they've been demolished to make way for the construction in progress of the government-sponsored eco-lodge. The main feature completed so far is a pier in the shape of a sleek motor yacht thrusting its bow into the blue waters of the lake. What else is there to do then? Endeshew, probably as of result of his 17 years of study at the monastery, proves a versatile guide. He suggests a 60-minute boat ride to Emperor

Susenyos' ruined palace which rises on the tip of the Mangai peninsula. Scott is immediately sold, "What better way is there to see Lake Tana than getting on a boat." I'm a little skeptical — an hour each way on a small open boat bumping on the waves and in the blazing tropical sun. But then Endeshew leads us to a long blue motor launch that is moored nearby, comfortably seating 20 passengers and with a striped awning to shield them from the sun. All for the round-trip price of 400 Birr or $8. In minutes we're aboard and underway.

As we travel along the rocky shore with its vegetation parched but still present at the height of the dry season, I'm reminded of another tropical African lake, one that I grew up with. Lake Malawi dominates with its size in the same way that Lake Tana does. Both stretch beyond the horizon, their blue waters make them seem like an inland ocean. Both offer a bounty to fishermen. We pass their papyrus canoes stacked upright against a tree on a small rocky island. A lone fisherman slowly paddles one probably towards a favored fishing spot. The 17th century French explorer Poncet confessed he couldn't fathom what kept them afloat. "Although the rushes of these boats are platted very tightly, yet I cannot conceive how these boats can be proof against water."[39] But what makes Lake Tana unique is its islands. 36 of them are occupied by either monasteries or churches. As we cruise towards one, Scott tells me that Graham Hancock's quest to find out what happened to the Ark of the Covenant once the Jews from Elephantine reached Lake Tana, led him to an island called Tana Qirqos. There, the monks, now Christians but originally Jews, showed him an ancient structure which they said once housed the Ark before King Azana's army arrived to take it to its new and final home in Axum.

Drawing level with the island I notice a telltale round church roof and a cluster of other modest buildings peeking through fig trees and other foliage. Some of these monasteries date back to the 14th century, Endeshew tells us, and have served as refuges for people and for ancient church manuscripts. Scott is more excited than I've seen him on the trip so far by the prospect of visiting one. But our first objective is to see Emperor Susenyos' palace.

---

[39] Charles-Jacques Poncet, 'The Red Sea and Adjacent Countries at the close of the 17th Century,' edited by William Foster, The Hakluyt Society, 1949, p. 135.

Ahead I can make out its dark silhouette rising above the trees on what looks at first like an island. Our boatman steers us around to the side facing the shore. I soon see that it's in fact a long narrow peninsula. He maneuvers in close looking for a landing spot. A teenage boy grazing his cattle watches us and then motions us to move further to the right to avoid a thick clump of reeds. A flock of white waterbirds takes flight as the bow noses into shore.

For a second day in a row we begin hiking in the midday heat, only this time the climb is shorter and much less steep. The many low acacia thornbushes growing here mean you have to pick your way carefully. The first thing we see is a long, low stone wall. And then the remains of an arch supported by a steel brace, clearly a modern conservation attempt. The square recesses visible inside the vault look surprisingly European. It turns out that although it's called Susenyos' palace it was largely built for him by a Portuguese Jesuit, Pero Pais, more commonly known by the Spanish version of his name, Pedro Paez.[40] Inside a walled enclosure Paez built in 1606 what became the first Catholic church in Ethiopia. Paez first persuaded Susenyos himself, and then through him a few years later all of his subjects, to renounce their Ethiopian Orthodox faith in favor of Roman Catholicism. But the people rebelled, violently rejecting the emperor's decision. So, when Susenyos's son, Fasilides, came to the throne he immediately restored the Ethiopian Orthodox Church and banished the Jesuits from his empire. The palace here and its church were then largely destroyed by the local people. Like many ruins the appeal for me of this site is its remoteness and very ruined-ness. White stones form an arch and door frame around the main entrance. The remains of a column nestle at the base of a leafy plant in an empty room. Windows with white lintels frame the blue water of the lake. All of it speaks of great age and loss. As for Pedro Paez, though he failed to convert Ethiopia to Catholicism he did have one enduring legacy. He was the first European to discover that Lake Tana was the source of the Blue Nile, much to the chagrin of the later Scottish explorer, James Bruce.[41] But Bruce was the first to trace the river all the way to Khartoum where it joins the

---

[40] 'The Jesuits in Ethiopia (1609-1641): Latin Letters in Translation', 2017 edited by Wendy Belcher Chronology & Introduction to the Text by Leonardo Cohen, 2017, pp. 1-24.

[41] E.A. Wallis Budge, 'A History of Ethiopia: Nubia and Abyssinia,' 1928 (Oosterhout: Anthropological Publications, 1970), p. 397.

White Nile, and, as we shall see, he didn't leave Ethiopia without another important trophy and bragging rights of his own.

Back on the boat Endeshew proposes that we make another stop on our return trip to Gorgora. Scott's earlier questioning has drawn from him an intriguing story about the role these island monasteries have played. Many have been used like bank safes, as secure repositories for valuable manuscripts. Sometimes, to provide an added layer of security against thieves, those manuscripts are rotated between monasteries on different islands. One of four that take part in this secret practice is Mandaba Medhanealem. As we discover when our boat docks, this monastery, like Susenyos' palace, is also built on a peninsula making it relatively easy to seal off from the mainland.[42]

At the main gate we are asked to show IDs. Not what I was expecting at a monastery founded in the 14th century! But after Kebrom shows his and talks to the guard, we are waved through. In front of the inevitable round church, newly restored with intricately carved wooden crosses on each of the shutters, is a small shrine to the founder, Abune Yasay. In contains a brightly colored portrait of him riding on a flat wooden raft across Lake Tana's blue waters. But looking closer we see the raft is the same shape as a flat, oval-shaped stone that's mounted in front of the painting. In Abune Yasay's hands this stone was transformed into the boat he used to travel the lake's waters. The Amharic phrase describing this miraculous transformation is *man inde aba* meaning "he who can do like the father." Hence the name of the monastery, Mandaba.

The monastery is a big one. 200 monks live here. We make our way through a maze-like mix of colorful vegetation and manmade structures, some ancient-looking like a stone cistern, others obviously recent like the simple dwellings made of corrugated iron. In front of one of these we encounter the senior monk who Endeshew wants to introduce us to. He alone can give us access to the monastery's collection of precious artifacts. Before Scott can even ask him what ancient manuscripts it contains, the monk begins addressing Kebrom. When he translates for

---

[42] Ethiopian Orthodox Tewahedo Church's Post. https://www.facebook.com/ETHOTC/posts/mandaba-man-ende-aba-medhanealem-unity-monastery-is-a-historical-monastery-found/835905625230345/

us, we learn that among its treasures is the original manuscript of the Book of Enoch, one of the lesser known biblical texts. Enoch is a mysterious antediluvian figure who some believe God carried up to heaven while still alive at the age of 365. His son, Methuselah lived even longer. Enoch also appears in three religions, Judaism, Christianity, and Islam.

On cue and like a conjurer, Scott pulls from his backpack his own personal copy of the Book of Enoch which he brought with him to Ethiopia for just such an occasion. The monk beams and inquires mischievously, "Is it a gift for me?" To which Scott offers an equally smart reply, "Well certainly, if you give me the original." The monk laughs and evades Scott's follow-up question — did the monastery provide a copy of the Book of Enoch to James Bruce which he took with him, thus re-introducing it to scholars in Europe? Instead, he tells us that thieves recently attempted to break into the building where the monastery's collection is housed. Fortunately, they failed but until a secure museum facility can be built, it will no longer be accessible to the public.

So unlike at Qusquam palace, where simply by requesting a key we were able to view the skeleton of Empress Mentewab and her illuminated manuscripts, there'll be no viewing of the treasures held here at Mandaba monastery. As we bid farewell to the senior monk and make our way back towards the monastery gate, we come across another round building made of corrugated iron. Only this one isn't a church, it's a kitchen. It's now 3pm, the hour when the Lenten fast is broken. From the kitchen emerges the enticing aroma of what we soon discover is something called *dabi*. *Dabi* is a thicker cousin of *enjera*, the traditional sponge-like flatbread eaten with most meals in Ethiopia. In addition to the monks themselves, visitors like us are invited to enjoy it slathered in a spicy relish. One of those visitors already munching on a piece of *dabi* between writing notes on his pad is Bitwoded Dagnew. He's an academic from the University of Gondar who is conducting a study of Ethiopian monasteries. As we begin talking, he nonchalantly delivers an astonishing fact: there are more than 400 monasteries still active in Ethiopia, most of them founded over four centuries ago. Perhaps at some point he can throw more light on Scott's unanswered question: from which of these and how did James Bruce manage to obtain his copy of the Book of Enoch?

As our boat pulls away towards Gorgora and we look up through the trees at the receding buildings of Mandaba monastery, Scott suddenly proclaims what sounds like an epiphany of his own, "You know, Ethiopia is really the Tibet of Africa." Almost on cue, after the boat docks and as we are looking for a place to buy some bottled water before we set off back to Gondar, we run into the 137-year-old monk living at the Debresina Mariam monastery who the abbot had told us about earlier in the day. Though not as old as Enoch he's still remarkably spry and has a wonderful smile. With an intricately decorated silver cross he blesses each of us and then the trunk and hood of Teddy's car to ensure a safe journey. It's a fitting end to the trip to Gorgora which so far has yielded disappointingly little to do with World War II. But what it has supplied are some dazzling and unexpected glimpses of Ethiopia's early imperial and spiritual history centered around the blue waters of Lake Tana.

On the way back to Gondar we find the turnoff to Genda. My hopes rise again. There's still a chance we can finish the day by discovering the Italian blockhouse whose capture marked the opening victory in the Gondar campaign. But after traveling less than a mile the road proves too rutted and rough for Teddy's Toyota to safely negotiate. Reluctantly we're forced to turn around. It's a good thing Kebrom has hired a 4-wheel drive vehicle for what promises to be the most critical day of my Gondar trip — attempting to retrace the path Sgt. Bruce Wickham and 54th Nyasaland took to reach their battle station for the attack on Gondar. As we near the city, the ring tone of birds twittering sounds from Kebrom's phone. "Hello." After a series of grunts, and then a burst of Amharic, he hangs up and turns. "We have our guards for tomorrow. Alemu and Yohannes have agreed to come with us again."

DAY FIVE — Friday, 3/17/23

Today could become a pivotal moment in my Gondar World War II expedition. The day when all my time spent pouring over the details of the 54th Nyasaland War Diary, and carefully matching the topography on Google Earth with that of the 54th artillery map — my "treasure map" as I've been calling it — could finally lead to the gold, to a moment and a place where history can be reborn.

At 8:30, a silver 4-wheel drive Toyota Landcruiser pulls up in front of our hotel driven by its proud owner Aschalo sporting shades and pencil moustache. Kebrom, my ever-reliable fixer, jumps out and taking me aside, quietly informs that we need to withdraw more money to cover what we're doing today. So before heading north out of the city we make a detour back to the bank on the old Viale Re Imperatore, Avenue of the King Emperor, where the March 1940 Italian newsreel showed crowds of cheering Italian settlers gathered to celebrate the progress made on Mussolini's "Second Rome."

But by November 1941 General Guglielmo Nasi and the 25,000 defenders who remained under his command were grimly hanging on, at the explicit orders of Il Duce. In a telegram Mussolini wrote words of encouragement to his commander. "Things are going very badly for the British in Europe. Russia staggers. Dear Nasi, resist until impossible, since the general situation is positive for the Axis. Let our flag fly over a strip of Empire until the day we reconquer it. Italy follows you and your soldiers with infinite admiration."[43] Mussolini wasn't simply boasting. The British were struggling to hold off Rommel's threat in North Africa. Apart from the port of Tobruk, now isolated, he had driven the British out of Libya and was preparing to invade Egypt itself. And by early November, Hitler's offensive against the Soviet Union, the largest in history with 3 million men, had advanced to within striking distance of Moscow.

---

[43] Angelo Del Boca, 'Gli Italiani in Africa Orientale Vol. 3 La caduta dell' impero,' 1982, p. 527.

The British, for their part, didn't see the capture of Gondar as a foregone conclusion. A War Office report describes Nasi as "the skillful commander who knew how to impose discipline on his men and made himself loved by the natives." That last quality was clearly an overstatement, but Nasi had done his best to boost morale in Gondar, even composing and popularizing a song called "I Gondarini" — We the Gondarini. One of the lines went "If you don't know us, let me tell you, we are the Gondarini, the die-hards."[44]

By then British air raids had become a daily hazard. Food was in short supply and expensive. Gondaree natives who could were fleeing the city to seek refuge in the surrounding countryside, among them Mulatu Wubneh's parents who, like us today, headed for the village of Ayba. British intelligence officers, scouting in forward positions for potential river crossings and passes through the mountains which made Gondar such a natural and formidable fortress, reported encountering refugees in groups, some as large as a hundred people.

At the traffic circle at the North end of Gondar, where the mountains start to grow steeper, Aschalo makes a stop to pick up Alemu and Yohannes, the same two guards who accompanied us up to Defecha Ridge and helped us find the ruined Italian fort. Alemu, the older of the two gives me a big grin as he climbs in the back, happy to be traveling in the comfort of the Landcruiser. Even Yohannes, always more reserved, runs his hand admiringly over the leather seat. The road we now take was originally built by the Italians more than 80 years ago. It's still the main access road to Gondar from the north. We climb and weave between rising peaks and deep valleys. It's easy to see why the British commander General Fowkes believed it would be a bloodbath if he tried to fight his way past the Italian defenses dug into the surrounding hilltops.

After 25 minutes, we're forced by a herd of goats to slow down while their owner moves them off to the side of the road. I calculate we're probably approaching the road section the Italians had blown up as a further deterrent against the attacking British forces. On the 54th Nyasaland artillery map it's indicated by a dotted line. A mile or two further on we enter the outskirts of the town of Amba

---

[44] Angelo Del Boca, 'Gli Italiani in Africa Orientale Vol. 3 La caduta dell' impero,' 1982, pp. 507 & 512.

Giorgis. Local Patriot forces had seized it several months before the campaign to take Gondar began. On the artillery map we've reached what's known as Kilometer 497, the distance the road had come from Asmara, the Eritrean capital. It's the place where the men of the 54th Nyasaland pitched their tents that first night at the end of a long grueling drive up from Massawa, the captured Red Sea port where they landed. Today their old roadside campsite is filled with densely packed houses made of corrugated iron, their roofs already heating up in the sun. At 9:20am we turn onto a dirt road heading south. I start my Garmin running watch in the bicycle mode, guessing it should most closely approximate our speed. According to the War Diary we should travel south for about 13 miles down what's described as the "Old Aiva track."[45]

Accounts vary on how this track came into being. Some say it was a mule trail, others, rather incredibly, that it was built by the Italians themselves but then neglected and forgotten. What is certain is that Ethiopian Patriot forces already operating in the area under British officers had discovered it and General Fowkes quickly saw it as a convenient way to bypass the strong Italian defenses his forces faced on the main road. Engineers from the Argyll and Sutherland Highlanders regiment had made it passable for military vehicles, explaining why on the 54th artillery map it's called 'Sutherland Lane.' Hundreds of mules and donkeys had also been commandeered from the surrounding countryside to carry munitions and supplies for the infantry battalions like the 2/2 KAR from Nyasaland who marched down it.

On Nov. 26, 1941, around 9am, the 54th Nyasaland Field Battery set off down this route. The 300 men, including my father, Sgt. Bruce Wickham, rode in trucks towing their eight guns and carrying all their ammunition and supplies. Eighty-two years later I find myself traveling down the same dirt road, literally following in his tracks. It's a magical and eerie feeling. At first, it's relatively smooth going through gently rolling countryside. There are even power lines alongside the road supplying the small farms we pass.

Before the Italian occupation, Ethiopia was still essentially governed by a type of feudal system. As historian Haile Larebo explained it, when we met for coffee

---

[45] Lt. Col. Hubert Moyse-Bartlett, The King's African Rifles Vol. 2, Ch. 21, p. 148/561 & p. 152/565ff.

once in Atlanta, most peasant farmers in the Amhara region owned their land, but they couldn't sell it, they could only pass it on to their children. They also had to share part of their crops or other goods with the nobility who governed the land. Today all land is owned by the Federal Government, it's one of the few reforms made by the Derg, the Marxist military regime that seized power in the 1970s, that has survived. Farmers can still use the land and pass it on to their children as before but now must pay an income tax to the government based on how much they produce. And, as when my father drove down this way, they still have no tractors only oxen to pull plows through the fertile but rocky soil. In a field off to one side I catch sight of a creature that brings back my own African childhood — a grivet monkey crouches, furtively eating something it has found while keeping a sharp eye out for scavengers that might try to steal it.

About 5 miles in, we come to a river. We can see that part of the concrete bridge has either collapsed or washed away. Aschalo steers us carefully down into the shallow riverbed itself. Then he engages his 4-wheel drive to climb the bank on the other side and head on into the first village we've seen. It's surrounded by the familiar forest of eucalyptus trees which provide timber for construction of all kinds, from barns to houses. I ask Alemu, who Kebrom has told me knows this area well, if this is Bambelo. I'd remembered the name from studying Google Maps. Alemu nods but then clarifies — that's the name of a nearby mountain; the village has a different name.

It dawns on me that we may be close to where my father and his 6-man gun crew got their first experience of battle. Three miles from the main road the 54th artillery map shows another track joining "Sutherland Lane." It weaves its way out to Argiv Ridge, a high point facing back west towards the mountains we've just driven through and where the Italian guns guarding the pass into Gondar were dug into the steep slopes. At the end of the 54th Nyasaland's long drive up from the coast, the War Diary states that General Fowkes, the Division commander, had ordered them "to be in action the following day."[46] So early on Nov. 17, the battery had driven out to begin positioning themselves just behind the brow of Argiv Ridge. The pressure to perform was on. Besides, Maj. Bingham, the 54th

---

[46] War Diary of 54th Nyasaland Field Battery Nov. 16-17, 1941, (See Appendix).

Nyasaland's commander, his superior Col. John Ormsby has also come to observe the unit. Sgt. Wickham may have known his way around a Bofors anti-aircraft gun but the 25-pound Mark 2 Howitzer — that, as Bingham recounts, he and his gun crew had labored to unload without proper gear and in sweltering heat from the ship's hold just days before — was a whole different animal. Sgt. Wickham had a six-man gun crew under his command, all Africans, most likely drawn from Bingham's initial group of KAR recruits. According to a chat group I'd found on WW2Talk, each man had a very specific role; (No. 1) breech operator/rammer, (No. 2) gun layer who sighted the gun, (No. 3) loader, (No. 4) ammunition handler, (No. 5) second ammunition handler who prepared the shells and set the fuses. (No. 6), usually a lance bombardier, served as second-in-command. It was now Sgt. Wickham's job to put his basic Chinyanja language skills to work and turn these six individuals into a well-oiled machine, capable of aiming, loading and firing up to two shells a minute. Luckily, they had plenty of ammunition, the battery had brought more than 1,500 rounds with them. By 2:30pm all 8 guns of the 54th Nyasaland Field Battery were aimed at three Italian targets, Crescent Hill, Larei and Ambazzo on the highest peak. On the call of "Fire", the guns went off. If was a deafening sound, probably the loudest these novice gunners had ever heard in their lives. An exhilarating and yet terrifying sound, a reminder that the original term for PTSD, Post Traumatic Stress Disorder, was a simpler and more intuitive one — "shell shock." And the guns' recoil mechanisms gave them a life of their own, kicking back the chamber as they sent their first high explosive shells of the war arcing towards the Italian positions. My father shouted a new command "Reload." He and his African gun crew were literally experiencing on-the-job training. For a battery that had only really come into existence in Nairobi six weeks ago it was a remarkable achievement. And they soon learned there was an enemy out there. Towards dusk Italian shells fell on Argiv Ridge but fortunately they suffered no casualties.

One gun soon developed a problem with its recoil mechanism, but some clever soldering by one of the mechanics took care of that. Over the next few days, the battery honed their skills. On Nov. 20th General Fowkes decided to pay them a visit. For the overall commander of the Gondar campaign a lot was riding on the effectiveness of his newest artillery unit so it's not surprising he wanted to see their capabilities for himself. Evidently, he must have been impressed by what he saw.

As Maj. Bingham, commander of the 54th Nyasaland, described it, in his oral history, "We spent our time shooting and shooting all day long until my soldiers were extremely proficient at pointing the guns in the right direction." Col. John Ormsby, the Royal Artillery commander, was also on hand to see the new battery in action. He'd worked hard to help secure the guns and personnel that were so urgently needed for the Gondar campaign. Afterwards he sent a telegram of congratulations that was read out to the men. By the morning of Nov. 26, when the battery set off down "Sutherland Lane" towards Ayba, they were ready.

As we come out of the village with the fork towards Argiv Ridge, I realize we've not seen a single vehicle since we left the main road, only people walking or herding cattle along the bumpy track. So, as we emerge into the next brown sweep of plowed fields, I'm surprised to see one off in the distance. It's a blue and white *bajaj*, Ethiopia's ubiquitous taxi, and it seems to have run into a problem. Its passengers stand forlornly on the side of the road although they manage to muster a smile and a wave as we pass. The driver is staring at his vehicle with a look of fierce concentration as though willing it to fix itself. A little further on a majestic view of the mountains we just passed through leaving Gondar opens up in front of us. We're soon traveling along the edge of a steep drop off.

In preparation for the trip, when I was looking for a modern topographical map to help me figure out the route my father would have taken, I'd emailed Kebrom to see if he knew of one. He said there weren't any but to try Google Earth. As soon as I did it led to a major revelation. From the 3D topographical display, I could see immediately that Ayba village where we're headed sits on a high plateau with a steep escarpment falling away to the west towards Gondar. As we now drive slowly along its edge, I see on the hillside opposite and below us scattered farms and one flat area with two circles. In the middle of those circles are posts where farmers can attach ropes to their oxen at harvest time as they drive them to thresh their wheat, separating the grain from the chaff. Many farmers still own only a single ox, so they depend on a contract system they call *mekenajo*, which enables them to time-share oxen belonging to their neighbors.[47]

---

[47] Atsabaha Gebre-Selassie, Tessema Bekele 'A Review of Ethiopian Agriculture: Roles, Policy and Small-scale Farming Systems' Global Growing Casebook, p. 56.

With my Garmin watch showing 10 miles we pull into the village which Alemu announces is Kagra. This is as far as Aschalo's skilled driving, and 4-wheel drive vehicle can take us. Clearly the track ahead has deteriorated since my father's day. Thanks to the handiwork of the Sutherland Highlander engineers it had been made passable enough for the 54th Nyasaland's trucks and guns to travel down all the way to Ayba. For us though, we're back on foot, following a narrow rocky path with stone walls on each side. Alemu takes the lead at his usual brisk pace, AK-47 slung over one shoulder.

Walking is actually better. I can feel the landscape, see up close the same fields and isolated trees my father and his fellow soldiers would've passed traveling the last few miles to Ayba. It was late November so they may have seen villagers harvesting crops. Their destination is marked on the artillery map as 'Campbell O.P.' short for Observation Post. Campbell was the name of the British officer commanding a group of Shoa Patriots who'd been sent ahead to hold the area. Those Patriots had come all the way from Addis Ababa, a distance of 400 miles. Some may even have watched Emperor Haile Selassie make his triumphal entry back into Addis Ababa earlier that year, sporting the long dreadlocks they'd vowed not to cut until the emperor's return.

After about a mile in the dusty heat, we see a man with a headscarf leaning against a rock wall up ahead, with him is a teenage boy wrapped in a blanket. When we reach them, we learn the Ayba village priest Kebrom has been in touch with has sent them to meet us and accompany us on the final stretch. Soon we see another group waiting at the edge of a large field. We shake hands with Father Abera, the priest in his white turban and another man who, like Alemu and Yohannes, is dressed in camouflage and nonchalantly clasping an AK-47. He's the local administrator, Sema Yedresew. Father Abera points and tells me through Kebrom that the large expanse of unusually flat fields behind him is where the British forces camped. It's called "Jambo." Tellingly Jambo is not an Amharic word, but in Swahili it means "hello." Most likely the East African soldiers who Bingham had commandeered in Kenya to fill out the 54th Nyasaland's ranks had used that greeting when they met the villagers of Ayba and the name has been preserved to this day. Our own warm reception also makes me remember my return to another African village, some 30 years ago, and how I was welcomed by an astonished then smiling Nickson Ndau, the man who taught me as a child how to make and fire my first catapult. And now here I am standing near the place where my father and his African crew were called upon to prove they could accurately fire their much bigger and more deadly weapon.

After delivering his initial greeting, Father Abera invites us to follow him. He leads the way past a small tree-covered hill and on towards the edge of the escarpment. "It's where the British positioned their guns," he says. 54th Nyasaland arrived here in the late afternoon on Nov. 26, 1941. By 5:30pm once they had dug in their eight guns behind a protective wall of sandbags, they fired off several rounds towards Gondar, to register their targets for the following day.[48] General Nasi, who by now had received reports of the latest British troop movements, ordered his artillery on Defecha and several other ridges to fire back. According to the War Diary, several rounds landed close to 54th Nyasaland's position but again they suffered no casualties. That night the British commander, General Fowkes, sent out a final message to his troops, "Tomorrow we put all to the test by general attack on Gondar. The enemy has shown courage and endurance, but we too can show ferocity and fortitude."[49] Where Fowkes would position himself during the battle the following day was still a mystery I needed to solve. I presumed it was on some high ground where he could observe the attack and be in radio contact with his field commanders to make any final adjustments to his battle plan should they prove necessary.

As we continue to walk with Father Abera, I notice other Ayba villagers are joining the procession. Soon a crowd of some 20 people are walking with us. I feel like the Pied Piper and hope that they, and I, won't be disappointed. The ground rises ahead as we approach the edge of the escarpment, and I notice a tree covered hill on our left. Mentally I'm reviewing the one photograph I have of my father's gun troop, its four 25-pounder howitzers slanting back in a row across a grassy plain with a hill behind on the right. That hill I'm seeing now could well be the one. It feels like I'm about to realize a dream the first glimmers of which appeared to me more than three years ago when I discovered this photo along with the studio

---

[48] War Diary of 54th Nyasaland Field Battery Nov. 26, 1941, (See Appendix).
[49] Lt. Col. Hubert Moyse-Bartlett, 'The King's African Rifles,' Vol. 2, Ch. 21, pp.152/565.

portrait of my father and his three fellow sergeants looking directly at me, dressed in their tropical military uniform.

Suddenly I hear someone shouting behind us. It gets louder. I have an ominous feeling in my stomach. Is my dream about to be snatched away at the last minute? Or worse still, like John Reed encountering those two guards on the road outside St. Petersburg, is my life about to be threatened? I turn and see the shouting is coming from another armed militia man dressed in camouflage who is shoving people aside to get to the front of the crowd. Alemu and Yohannes, our two guards, immediately move towards him, calmly taking up a position between Scott and I and the agitated man. Kebrom joins them and listens. Gradually the shouting subsides. The man is speaking now in a more normal voice, although clearly still angry. He wants to know what's going on, why hasn't he been informed about these strangers suddenly showing up in his district. I notice Father Abera, the priest, talking urgently on his cell phone. Then he walks over and hands it to Kebrom who listens intently. Alemu and Yohannes continue to position themselves between Scott and I and the irate guard who's still glaring at everyone.

After a few minutes, Kebrom calmly addresses him. Whatever he says appears to placate the man. Once again we can proceed towards the edge of the escarpment where the British guns would most likely have been positioned. But as we approach the spot the priest, Father Abera, suddenly points his staff up at the hill on our left and begins moving towards it. Clearly, we must follow along with the rest of the crowd, now grown to about 30, including old men shuffling along with sticks and several young boys, one boisterously dodging in and out of the climbing grown-ups. Now I see why Father Abera has brought us up to this elevated spot. In front of me is a sweeping view of what was to be the battlefield on Nov. 27, 1941.

Surrounded by expectant faces, I fumble in my backpack for my compass and a list of bearings as well my father's binoculars. I scan the landscape in front of me. No sign of Debre Birhan, the church we visited two days ago, but that's probably because it's hidden behind Defecha Ridge. And then I spot it, a round pink circle. It's the roof of Defecha Kidanemihret church where we stopped at the crown of the ridge. Instantly it's the sun around which the other constellations revolve: to the left is the southern end of Defecha Ridge with its fort, artillery and machine guns, further to the left is the bare summit of Gantz Hill, 54th Nyasaland's forward observation post. To the right is Deva Ridge where the Italian guns could be pulled back into caves. I hand the binoculars to Kebrom so he can see the key landmarks and relay them to the crowd pressed around us. The compass bearing on Debre Birhan looks right too, I tell him, close to 289 degrees, although I can't really see the church. It's time to document the long-anticipated moment with some photos. We all sit down on brow of the hill while Kebrom and Scott both click away. The agitated militia man continues to hold himself aloof from the celebration, watching sullenly and silent. Out of the corner of my eye I catch him taking his aggressions out on the young boy who's been happily horsing around through the crowd. He suddenly hurls a small rock at the boy, striking him on the side of the head and drawing some blood. But no one seems to see this as anything unusual.

The crowd looks ready to move on, so I quickly announce I need to go back down the slope we'd scrambled up to take some photos down below as well. I know this hill is too steep for the 54th Nyasaland to have hauled their heavy guns and gear up here. Besides, the photo I have — possibly, I now realize, the only photo that exists of the entire battle of Gondar — shows them dug in behind sandbags in a grassy field. Back down on the flat saddle area I find a likely spot with the hill to the right matching that photo. Looking into the distance I spot something else, a peak poking up just above the horizon, also in the photo.

I grab several rocks and pile them into a small cairn to mark the spot. Stepping back, I take a couple of shots. As best as I can tell this is the place where my father and the 54th Nyasaland positioned their guns for the battle that would finally liberate Gondar and Ethiopia some 80 years ago.

Satisfied, I scramble back up the hill where the Ayba villagers are patiently waiting. We continue along the edge of the ridge. The major shortcoming of the artillery map has always been that the gun position marked as Campbell O.P. sits in the middle of a conspicuously blank spot. Hastily putting it together just days before the battle, the mapmakers had no topographical data for this area. But seeing the steepness of the escarpment sloping down towards Gondar, it's clear to me that 54th Nyasaland had to have stayed up here on the ridge. There's no way their trucks and guns could have gone down the escarpment. In fact, one puzzling detail from one of the War Diaries now makes perfect sense. It records how the second artillery unit, the 22nd Indian Mountain Battery, which was armed with smaller caliber guns, swapped its vehicles for mules. The guns were taken apart and loaded onto the animals' backs so that they could take up a position closer to Gondar and also act as a forward observation post for 54th Nyasaland. As they descended the escarpment three of the mules lost their footing and fell to their deaths. Looking at a narrow footpath slanting away down the mountainside in front of us I can easily see how it happened. Then shifting my gaze off into the distance, to the ridges defending Gondar, I can for the first time appreciate the art of "indirect fire" that my 24-year-old father and his African gunners had to master. When their forward observers had called for "rapid fire" to stop the devastating machine-gun and artillery fire raining down on their own infantry as they scrambled up Defecha Ridge, they'd swiveled their gun one or even half a degree. Then after quickly dialing in distance and trajectory for a target six miles away which they most likely couldn't see, they had rained down 9 or 10 high explosive shells in six minutes on an Italian fort, the same Italian fort whose blackened ruins I'd found and walked through just two days ago.

We continue along the Ayba ridge to where it begins to drop back down to a lower elevation. Beyond I can see the feature that I previously dubbed the decapitated pyramid and initially thought the most likely position for 54th Nyasaland. But it now looks too far south and there's no sign of any track leading there. As a way of thanking the villagers for acting as guides, I end our journey together by sharing my father's personal story and showing them the photos I have of him and his three fellow sergeants and of the guns they set up in the grassy field on Ayba Ridge. Kebrom interprets and displays the photographs. While the older men nod and talk, I notice one teenager peering intently at the black and white images, as if to assure himself that all this is real and not some white foreigner's harebrained fantasy.

When it's over, at Father Abera's invitation, we head back downhill towards the Ayba village church. It's another 20-minute hike. Across an expanse of fields, a stream the dry season has reduced to a trickle and up the slope beyond it. We pass tin-roofed farmhouses with mounds of cow patties stacked outside for fuel and eventually arrive at the church enclosed as usual by a stone wall and a clump of trees. Coincidentally, this one, like the one on Defecha, is also called Kidanemihret, Place of Mercy.

Although intended to provide mercy, this church once witnessed a grizzly atrocity. According to one member of the congregation who steps forward to tell the story, during the occupation the Italians established a store here. He points to a stone building nestled behind a nearby wall. But either the local priest would not give his permission or else he angered them in some other way. As a reprisal the Italians killed him and then hung his body from one of the trees around the church.

There's one final part to the man's horrific tale. After lynching the priest, the Italians then tried to set fire to the church but were driven away by a swarm of bees. This detail has a familiar ring to it. The same thing happened to the 1888 Mahdist attackers at Debre Birhan church. Was it a miracle? Or a metaphor for the priest and his rural community's defiant refusal to become an Italian colony? Mussolini's ambition for Amhara province, which he personally sponsored, was for 1,000 settler families to take ownership of nearly 150,000 acres in the first 6 years. But according to historian Haile Larebo, in his detailed study of Mussolini's attempt to build his East African empire, the effort fell far short. This was primarily because local armed resistance in the region was so strong, bottling up the Italian occupiers in a few urban areas and settler camps where "each group of four houses was protected by barbed wire and machine guns. Every Sunday the farmers received combat training in the use of hand grenades and automatic weapons."[50] The ferocity of local resistance is perhaps best explained by an Ethiopian proverb, "To be landless is to be subhuman."

On this somber note, our visit to Ayba seems to have run its course. I have no sense of how much time has passed since we set out on foot from Kagra village. Somewhere between a few minutes and an eternity. But my Garmin watch tells me we've covered 3.5 miles. With the 10 miles we drove that brings us close to the 13 I was expecting. The militia man who was so incensed by our presence as parting gesture apologizes for his earlier outburst. He even accompanies us part of the way as we head back, passing once again Jambo field where Father Abera, the village priest, told us 54th Nyasaland had pitched their tents.

My father and his 300 fellow soldiers would spend another night there at the end of a day in which they'd managed to destroy or at least neutralize all the Italian

---

[50] Haile Larebo, 'The Building of an Empire: Italian Land Policy & Practice in Ethiopia, in Ethiopia, 1935-1941,' p. 157 & 161.

defenses they fired at. In World War II, as I'd come to realize visiting Ayba, gunners were the nerds of the military. They had to master dial sights, fire directors and inclinometers and they had to become expert map readers who could accurately translate its contours into the 3-dimensional landscape in front of them. With the help of their precision firing, my father and his comrades knew that by 2pm 2/2 KAR, the infantry battalion made up of their fellow Nyasalanders, had taken Defecha Ridge and that by 4pm 4/4 KAR, another infantry unit from Uganda, had taken their third target, Maldiba Ridge which rose next to it to the south. They must also have heard that Gondar itself had surrendered. For most of the battery, including my father this was their first taste of war. Whether they celebrated or simply felt relieved I do not know. In other circumstances, the gunners from Nyasaland might have staged an *ngoma*, a celebration with songs and generous quantities of maize beer. Here they might at least have struck up a song of home, "The country of Nyasaland, wouldn't it be fine to be there."[51] The battery as a whole certainly took pride in what they had done. The final note in the War Diary that day reads "Enemy did not try to engage the Battery position throughout the action." This also reveals something new to me about my father. By developing an expertise as gunner he'd found a way to fight a war effectively while still keeping himself far from harm's way, unlike the infantryman on the front line.

By the time we reach Aschalo and his Landcruiser we've walked 6 miles. But to someone who's run several marathons it feels like 26.2, the end of an epic journey. In the process I feel like I've traveled into a different dimension, one where I've caught a few vivid glimpses of the world my 24-year-old father inhabited along with the three nameless sergeants who appear in the photo I have of him. A world they shared with their African gunners, who made up the majority of 54th Nyasaland, and of whom I have neither images nor names. I've seen where they positioned and fired their guns and I've met the descendants of the people of Ayba whose village they liberated from Italian colonial oppression and where life today, apart from the cell phones and AK-47 rifles, remains remarkably unchanged. As

---

[51] Timothy J. Lovering, 'Authority And Identity: Malawian Soldiers in Britain's Colonial Army 1891-1964,' Doctoral Thesis U. of Sterling, pp. 221-222 & 260.

Scott, in his wry, laconic way, summed up the experience, "It certainly beats going on a cruise."

When we reach the road to Gondar that winds back through the mountains, where a few isolated Italian artillery units still held out for another day, one more discovery awaits me. Kebrom tells us we must stop at a place called Wunania. There's something he wants to show us. As we pull over to the side of road and walk a few steps, a Grand Canyon-like spectacle opens up under our feet. We're literally standing on the edge of the Ethiopian Highlands, where a panoramic display of geological majesty and mayhem sculpted over millions of years unfolds in front of us. A dark volcanic plug rears its head below us as other peaks march off to the horizon. I suddenly realize that this is where the fourth wartime photograph I have from my father was taken. Perhaps, like us now, he took it on his way into Gondar which he would finally see in person two weeks after the Italian surrender. It seems a fitting place to take a photo with Alemu and Yohannes, our guards. Although I don't yet know it, they will provide an unexpected link between my father's war and the one that has only just ended in Ethiopia today.

DAY SIX — Saturday, 3/18/23

When Kebrom dropped us off at the hotel last night I told him we'd take it easy today. Have a late morning start and maybe visit a museum if there is one. I wanted to spend some time reviewing what seems like a flurry of discoveries so I could share them with "the Professor" who'd done so much to make this trip possible. As it's the weekend, Mulatu has no classes to teach so I've invited him to join us.

Since the 54th artillery map has been my main guide, I decide to start there. After standing on Ayba Ridge on the exact spot where the guns were positioned, I now have a clear picture of what my father could see in front of him on the morning of Nov. 27, 1941. I follow the range line drawn on the map to the 54th Nyasaland's nearest target; the south end of Defecha Ridge. Through persistence, and even though Alemu insisted we were on Maldiba not Defecha, we'd managed to locate the remains of the Italian stone fort whose artillery and machine guns had at first cut to pieces the 54th Nyasaland's fellow soldiers in the 2/2 KAR infantry. They'd also been hit by Italian guns on Deva Ridge, just to the north. Those guns had been a harder target to strike. After firing a barrage their Italian gunners could pull them back inside some caves for cover. Unfortunately, Kebrom had told me early on that Deva Ridge would be extremely hard to reach. All the more frustrating because he said the caves most likely also contained a church which sounded intriguing to both Scott and me.

The range lines on the map between Defecha and Deva are bisected by the line to what is clearly 54th Nyasaland's most difficult target. At 15,500 yards, it is almost 9 miles away. When General Nasi realized the main British attack would come from the East instead of the North, he ordered one of his heaviest artillery batteries defending the Ambazzo Pass to move to this new position called Dunquam Hill.

By late morning, those repositioned Italian guns were causing new problems for 2/2 KAR infantry attacking Defecha Ridge. 54th Nyasaland received an urgent call from their forward observers to redirect their fire at Dunquam Hill. Clearly proud of their accuracy at extreme range, the officer in charge had written on the 54th artillery map "Enemy 77mm, 3 guns, silenced with 19 rounds." Mulatu had suggested during our planning session on the first day that Dunquam was likely a misreading of Qusquam. Which is why we visited the palace there. And his theory was supported by our guide Abebe, who explicitly said the palace had been heavily damaged by British artillery. But now as I look again more closely at this part of the artillery map something I'd missed catches my eye. Faintly marked and a bit lower down I now make it out — "Cusquam monastery." The first letter in Amharic can be transliterated as either Q, C or K. This means Qusquam can't be Dunquam after all. They were two separate places. The problem is that Dunquam Hill, just like 54th Nyasaland's gun position on Ayba Ridge, appears in a topographical blank spot on the map, just above a place called Gonderac Giorgis.

I decide to take another look at Google Earth. I quickly find a church with a similar spelling called Gonderoch Giorgis. Next to it is a wooded hill, unnamed but certainly a possible candidate for Dunquam Hill. When Kebrom arrives at the hotel I alert him to my discovery. Pulling up Google Earth on his phone, he says he can see a road going there and, even better news, one passable by *bajaj*, so no need for another expensive 4-wheel drive excursion. Since it's out in countryside, we will of course need to take our guards, Alemu and Yohannes, if they are available. He says he'll try to set it up for tomorrow.

By the time "the Professor" arrives, Kebrom has already heard back from Alemu. He and Yohannes are on for Dunquam Hill tomorrow. Mulatu is beaming as he walks into the hotel lobby. Wearing a baseball cap and hiking boots he's clearly ready for some outdoor action. "So, you had a successful to trip to Ayba," he says, obviously having been tipped off by Kebrom. "Yes," I say, "Half the village came out to greet us and then accompany us to the spot."

Bajaj taxis are designed for a maximum of three passengers; all wedged into the back seat. So, this time we hail two for our ride to the museum that Kebrom has picked out for us to visit. I ride with Mulatu so I can tell him more about our amazing Ayba adventure as well as today's revelation that Dunquam isn't Qusquam after all. The route to the museum is by now a familiar one — the main divided highway for the first 10 minutes and then climbing and dodging through the crowded cobbled streets that bring us to Fasil Ghebbi, the Castle Enclosure. A few more minutes and we arrive outside the museum entrance. It isn't what I was expecting at all. It's housed in another grand Gondaree palace.

But we have to wait for Scott and Kebrom to arrive before we can go inside. To pass the time Mulatu and I look at a stall outside the museum entrance run by a woman selling herbs. One of the items she's carefully laid out is a type of grass. Mulatu explains that it's used as part of the coffee ceremony. Then, his botanical curiosity clearly aroused, he asks the woman if she has any *endod*, the herb that kills bilharzia, also known as schistosomiasis, a snail-born disease that infects many of Africa's lakes and is second only to malaria in its deadly effect. Growing up in Malawi it had been drummed into me from an early age — don't go into any water, particularly stagnant pools. No, the herbseller doesn't have any *endod* but then without a word she disappears off down the street to find some. While we wait Mulatu points to the church opposite. "That's the one that has the caves in the embankment below which people used as bomb shelters during the war." It was the same one we'd passed on our first day with Kebrom. When he was a child, Mulatu's mother had told him a friend of hers, a woman, had been killed by a British bomb exploding right in front of the cave entrance, as she was about to go inside. After hearing about this tragedy, she and his father decided it was time to leave the city. Just then the woman from the herb stall comes back triumphantly bearing a bunch of the bilharzia-killing herb. Carefully taking it and examining it, Mulatu explains that it was discovered in the 1960s by Aklilu Lemma, an Ethiopian doctor who noticed it growing in some water where women were washing clothes, using the suds it produces as a type of natural detergent. Besides cleaning clothes, what the doctor soon observed was that it also killed the snails that carry the bilharzia parasite. Mulatu clearly revels in the unexpected and beneficial cures derived from Nature, especially one discovered by a fellow Ethiopian. By then Kebrom and Scott have arrived in their *bajaj* and we go on through the stone gate of the museum.

Its full title is Ras Ghimb Museum, meaning Prince's Palace. In the middle of its park-like grounds surrounded by trees, it rises like a small version of Emperor Fasilides' much larger stone palace in the castle enclosure. There's some debate over whether Fasilides built it as a prototype for his palace or whether it came sometime later.

Today it's become almost a time capsule of Ethiopian history. As our guide tells us, early on it served as the residence of Ras Mikael Sehul, the Tigrayan prince who we've come to know already as a key player in the mounting power struggles in Gondar during the second half of the 18th century.[52] It's a period Ethiopians call Zemena Mesafint — the Era of the Princes. One the objects belonging to Ras Mikael is a large, ornate pewter dish. When our guide next tells us it was a gift from the Scottish explorer James Bruce, Scott's curiosity is immediately aroused. The plate is covered with botanical etchings, some even look like thistle flowers, the emblem of Scotland, Bruce's homeland. Examining it closely Scott suspects it must be the present Bruce gave Ras Mikael at their first meeting arranged by the letter of introduction sent by his wife, Aster. When he was admitted to see the prince in one of the rooms here, Bruce found a man as tall as himself but much older, with curly white hair and sharp, alert eyes. When he requested a guarantee of his safety during his visit, the Prince gave a frank and chilling response: "Other countries are not like this, though this was never so bad as it is now. These wretches here are enemies to strangers; if they saw you alone in your own parlor, their first thought would be how to murder you; though they knew they were to get nothing by it, they would murder you for mere mischief." Ras Mikael was alluding to the unusually violent times Ethiopia was going through. Just days before he'd returned from battle and put on a ghastly public spectacle for Gondar's citizens. He'd ordered that ten chiefs taken prisoner first have their eyes gouged out, then be dragged out into the fields and left to be eaten by hyenas. Bruce had himself witnessed the grisly scene.[53]

But Bruce was probably counting on the fact that Ras Mikael felt deeply indebted to him for the lifesaving work he'd already performed up at Qusquam palace. As I'd learned during our visit there, Bruce had managed to cure a number of Ras Mikael's and his wife Aster's family, including their youngest child, who'd been stricken with smallpox. Since the Scot had also shown he was both an accomplished horseman and marksman, Ras Mikael decided to make him commander

---

[52] Bahru Zewde, 'A History of Modern Ethiopia, 1855-1991,'(2001), p. 11.

[53] James Bruce, 'Travels to Discover the Source of the Nile (1790 edition), Vol. 3, Book 5, Ch. 8, pp. 216-229.

of the Koccob ["star" in Amharic] cavalry, an honorary position in the emperor's household that should serve as a deterrent to any would be attackers. To further emphasize his gratitude to Bruce, his parting words to him were: "Yagoube, [Ethiopian for James] it will take a long day to settle that account with you."

More than a century later, the new powerbrokers in Gondar, its Italian occupiers, restored Ras Ghimb, which like most of Gondar's royal buildings had fallen into disrepair, and turned it into offices for the senior military staff. The ground floor meeting room is filled with high quality wooden furniture from that era.

In the second half of the twentieth century, Ras Ghimb reverted to being what it was originally intended to be: an imperial palace. The second floor houses the bedrooms and bathrooms equipped with wonderfully elaborate and now antique bidet and shower fixtures for Haile Selassie and his wife. After Haile Selassie was overthrown by the Marxist military regime known as the Derg, they turned what was the chapel into a torture chamber.

But the most intriguing room at Ras Ghimb still awaits us at the very top of the building. As we come out onto the roof with its stone battlements and round domes at the corners that served as guards' quarters, my eye is drawn to the view to the East. Above the roofs of Gondar looms Ayba Ridge where I stood just yesterday. Its sheer bulk is menacing and it's obvious what a strategic advantage it gave my father's artillery unit on the morning of the attack. They could clearly see the roofs of Gondar through the sights of their guns.

Behind me, our guide beckons to us to come and see something else. She leads us up a staircase, that is normally kept roped off to the public. It leads to a small room in the palace tower. On one side are bookshelves filled with reference books in Italian. This was the Italian administration's library. Mulatu, who has made a detailed study of Italian urban planning in Gondar, never even knew it existed. On the opposite side are a series of illustrations of Gondar history, including a painting by an unnamed Ethiopian artist depicting in a primitivist style the battle of November 27, 1941. In the top half, colored in light pastels, the British attackers are shown as combined European and African troops, led rather incongruously by tanks, while the Italian defenders are depicted as a dense pack of white riflemen behind a stone wall. In the lower half of the painting the surrender of General Nasi is taking place. He salutes the British commander who is wearing a Scottish-style cap while African guards with rifles look on menacingly. To the left the Ethiopian and British flags are raised over Emperor Fasilides' castle. In this painting no artillery is depicted, but in a similar painting perhaps by the same artist, two white gunners and a white officer, looking through binoculars, are shown manning a single gun.[54] In fact, as I've discovered, most of the men in 54th Nyasaland Field Battery were Africans, mainly from modern-day Malawi but also from Kenya and Uganda. As far I know these and my father's photo of his four-gun troop out on Ayba Ridge are among the few images that exist of the Battle of Gondar.

As we are about to leave the Ras Ghimb Museum, with its grim themes of war and the struggle for power over the centuries, we're treated to an unexpected and welcome burst of sheer joy. A woman wearing a brightly colored scarf of blue, pink, and gold and uttering a lilting stream of Amharic suddenly runs up to Kebrom and embraces him. It's his old high school teacher who hasn't seen him for years and remembers him as one of her favorite students.

By now, it's technically lunch time. Although to cope with the fasting for Lent by everyone around us Scott and I have given up on lunch and switched to eating a hearty breakfast and dinner. So, when Mulatu suggests we try a favorite restaurant of his near Fasil Ghebbi I'm completely caught off guard. "But I thought you couldn't eat till three." Mulatu proceeds to explain that, in the Ethiopian Orthodox Church, Lent lasts not 40 days but 55 days. But those extra days don't make it longer, they're just to make up for the weekend days. Because on the weekend you take a break from fasting. It's still 40 days total but not all at once. Like the spontaneous handling of the traffic jam on way to Gorgora, this peculiarly Ethiopian custom seems a very practical and humane one.

Fasil Lodge, the restaurant Mulatu has in mind, suddenly presents itself as an oasis of calm amid the blaring of *bajaj* horns and the roar of traffic around Gondar's Castle Enclosure. We enter through an avenue of trees and shrubs that sets it back from the street and soothingly muffles the city's din. We are greeted by the owner, Efrem. I notice some of the greenery we passed has red berries on it. Efrem says they're coffee beans and then, grasping a few on a branch, he proceeds to tell us the legend of how coffee was discovered in Ethiopia. A sheep herder named

---

[54] Ethiopian painting depicting the Battle of Gondar, Museum of Fine Arts, Boston. https://collections.mfa.org/objects/503016

Kaldi noticed how his goats sometimes remained frisky and alert when they returned from grazing. They also appeared to need very little sleep. One day he decided to follow them to see what they were eating. He saw that they liked to reach up for the berries on a certain bushy tree. So, Kaldi decided if it makes goats feel alert and stay awake maybe I should give it a try. And that's how coffee came into the world. Sometime later, Kaldi shared his secret with a monk who kept falling asleep during prayers but now found with coffee he could pray for twenty-four hours straight.

While Kebrom and Mulatu go off to eat their first hearty lunch in five days, Scott and I decide to partake in the Ethiopian coffee ritual. Behind a fringe of the same grass the woman was selling outside Ras Ghimb, the coffee brewer, a young woman in a green dress with a white sash, seats herself on a low stool behind what looks like a coffee altar, a carved wooden chest whose lid is covered with small white cups. She begins roasting the beans over burning coals beside her. She then grinds and brews them. Finally, she brings the cups and an incense burner to our table. After first putting a spoonful of sugar in each cup, she pours the coffee from a black pot. The narrow spout allows her to pour the coffee from about a foot above the cup. It descends in a thin stream without spilling a drop. The incense wafts through the air as we sip the coffee and, in what seems a surprising, almost American touch, munch on popcorn.

Conspicuously absent from the World War II painting we saw at Ras Ghimb and also from the battle sites connected to my father and the 54th Nyasaland is one group who played an important role in the liberation of Gondar. The gatekeeper at Debre Birhan church who told us about the British shell that exploded against the outer wall gave us a small hint of their existence. He'd heard the story from his father who fought as a Patriot under the command of the Ethiopian leader Fitaurari Birru. The Ethiopians called them the *Arbegnoch*, Patriots or Resistance fighters. By November 1941 the ranks of the Patriots had swelled to include groups of Ethiopians who had originally fought with the Italian Army as Colonial troops known as *Askari* or as supporting militias known as *Banda*. Our task for the afternoon with Mulatu's help is to go in search of the route that brought one of these Patriot groups so rapidly and unexpectedly to the center of the city in the culminating hours of the battle.

We set off along east wall of Fasil Ghebbi, first passing two churches that are inside the wall. As we walk, Mulatu shares a new piece of information about Efrem, the affable restaurant owner. His maternal grandfather was a Patriot leader named Dejazmach Arayia. His group fought 60 miles north of Gondar against the Italian garrison at Wolchefit, which for months held off the British forces that were trying to come up the only road leading to up to the Grand Canyon-like edge of the Ethiopian Highlands we'd stood on at the end of our expedition to Ayba. Eventually that garrison had been forced to surrender in late September 1941.

Walking along the east wall of the Castle Enclosure, the battles of World War II are temporarily pushed to the back of my mind by the striking images from Gondar's deeper past. Ahead are two stone bridges arcing across the road. Each leads to one of the 12 gates that pierce the enclosure's outer wall. They have medieval-sounding names. The first is the Gate of the Spinners. To prevent a collapse, its bridge has been reinforced with a rather flimsy-looking metal brace. Beyond it is the Gate of the Chamberlain Turcurie, evidently a once famous court official. It too has a flimsy metal brace. Coincidentally, as we approach an old-fashioned horse-drawn carriage, now largely replaced by the *bajaj*, is passing under the old stone bridge.

Rounding the southern end of the Castle Enclosure wall we come to Jan Tekel, the small square with the giant sycamore tree where Emperor Fasililides first made camp, that we saw on our second day. Opposite the giant tree and itself half hidden by a row of trees is a nondescript two-story building. A blue sign outside announces that it houses the Gondar City Education Dept. But its faded yellow paint hints at an earlier function.

During the occupation the Italians built this as their new Town Hall. And around 4pm on November 27, 1941, it's where a momentous event took place. The Wollo Banda, one of the Patriot forces participating in the final attack, numbered less than 1,000 men. They were under the command of a British officer, Captain Mark Pilkington. Pilkington and the Wollo Banda became the first group to fight their way into city. And they weren't even supposed to be anywhere near here. General C.C. Fowkes when he drew up his battle plan believed it would take not one but two days to capture the city.[55]

Shortly before setting off on this trip to Ethiopia, I'd finally got access to a privately published book containing letters from Mark Pilkington as well as his liaison officer, Capt. Peter Molloy, during the Gondar campaign.[56] I became intrigued by him because I saw some resemblances to my father. He came from a similar though slightly more privileged background. He also had the same reserved yet easygoing character. But, unlike my father, he'd left behind an account of his experience in Ethiopia. With the help of his letters, I've been able to piece together the crucial part he and the Wollo Banda played on the day of the final attack.

By November 1941, Mark Pilkington had been fighting in Ethiopia for over six months, longer than almost every other British soldier on the battlefield that day. He came from an upper-class family — educated at Eton, then Oxford University, he even stood as a Conservative parliamentary candidate for East Woolwich. But then he traded a conventional life for something more out-of-the-box, leaving a strait-laced cavalry unit to join Major Orde Wingate's improvised guerrilla force. In spite of his shabby appearance with his wispy red beard and dirty old khaki sweater accompanied by what to some was an annoyingly vague and noncommittal manner, he'd proved himself a surprisingly effective and courageous leader, one who the Wollo Banda Patriots had grown to trust. A few months earlier when Pilkington ran out of money to pay his men — the accepted currency was Maria Theresa silver dollars that were due to be air dropped by the RAF — he made an impassioned plea to the battalion not to desert him, to trust that he would get them their wages. After listening in silence, they raised him on their shoulders and carried him into camp where each man shook his hand.[57]

November 27th, 1941, would be a new test. As Pilkington writes, "I was given a very strong position to attack, the line of forts guarding Azezo and the approaches to Gondar, and this time no support of any sort." Patriot forces were routinely treated as inferior to the British regular forces. Peter Molloy paints an even starker

---

[55] David Shirreff, 'Bare Feet and Bandoliers,' pp. 268-271.

[56] Mark Pilkington, *Some Letters, 1939-1942*, Printed by William Clowes & Sons, London & Beccles.

[57] David Shirreff, 'Bare Feet and Bandoliers,' pp. 243-244.

picture, "We were put on the right flank and had a series of obstacles between us and the city, which Brigadier James admitted to me afterwards, he was sure would prevent us getting there before his own troops." Molloy had to haggle for days just to get transport for their ammunition and to move the artillery support Pilkington's tough Irish sergeant, Morrow, had cobbled together from captured Italian guns.

Despite these handicaps, a little after 12pm, Pilkington radioed Molloy that he and Wollo Banda had managed to seize their objectives for the first day. An hour later Molloy's radio crackled to life again. "At 1300 hours Mark signaled me briefly, 'Am going on to Gondar.' I was flabbergasted. Not only was it contrary to orders, but he had 6 miles to go up an open, shallow valley, overlooked on both sides by Italian positions." Arriving outside Fasilides Castle, which served as the Italian military headquarters, Pilkington and the Wollo Banda took on the last Italian resistance standing in their way. "We were then in Gondar hours ahead of either of the regular African brigades! We had some fighting at the old Portuguese castle, where the carabinieri held out, but this was soon over, and I went off to see General Nasi. It was a great day for the Wollo Banda." Somehow Pilkington learned that the Italian commander, General Guglielmo Nasi, was across the street from the main Castle Enclosure in the Town Hall. So, no doubt with a contingent of Wollo Banda fighters acting as his bodyguard, he walked over and went inside.[58]

80 years later Mulatu, Scott, Kebrom and I follow in Pilkington's footsteps. The reception area is dark and empty. The paint on the yellow walls is peeling. Above the door on my right, I see a notice in English which reads "Welcome to the Coordinating Center." An education center employee working at his computer barely looks up at us. On the other side a dark hallway leads to some stairs to the second floor. Perhaps that's where Captain Pilkington and his Wollo Banda escort found General Nasi. Initially he refuses to surrender, perhaps he's stalling for time. Sensing the British were gaining the upper hand, Nasi had already sent out a pair of envoys to meet with Brigadier James, commander of the 25th Brigade, to explore terms for surrender. But within minutes a second British officer arrives. Major Yeatman, commander of a group of Kenyan armored cars, had raced into town

---

[58] David Shirreff, 'Bare Feet and Bandoliers,' pp. 270-271.

virtually unopposed. Since he outranks Pilkington and commands a regular British force, General Nasi agrees to surrender, handing over his sword to Yeatman.

Molloy, who was in frequent touch with 25th Brigade Headquarters all afternoon, writes, "What I know for certain is that Nasi's first offer to our Brigadier for an 'honorable surrender' was quickly followed by a second for an unconditional one, if only we could save the town from Mark's troops!"[59] Italian accounts, often without any proof, frequently described Patriot behavior as unpredictable and liable to turn violent. As a result, Capt. Pilkington, like Wingate before him, had learned he could put pressure on an enemy commander to surrender simply by suggesting he couldn't control how his Patriot forces might react if they didn't get their way. It seems likely he used the same tactic to persuade General Nasi to give in.

Back out in the sunshine that bathes Jan Tekel square, Kebrom hails two *bajajs*. Mulatu and I climb into the leading one. Heading south our goal is to try to reconstruct the route the fast-moving Wollo Banda would have taken to enter the city. As the name *banda* suggests they were originally a militia group fighting for the Italians who had switched sides. But these Wollo fighters weren't from Gondar, they came from an area further east. So how did these strangers and their British commander, Pilkington, find their way so quickly into the heart of Gondar?

As the *bajaj* heads south we leave behind the old Italian quarter of Gondar, entering what was called the indigenous quarter. At its center was Kidame Gebya, the Saturday market. It's still Gondar's main market but its labyrinth of stalls is now open every day. As we approach the bustle and milling crowds at the main entrance, Mulatu tells the driver to veer to the left. Almost immediately the buildings disappear and we're plunging downhill with a forest of eucalyptus on our right. "This road didn't exist back then," says Mulatu. "It was just a tree-covered mountainside with no paths even." At the bottom we come out at the edge of Addis Alem, the old Muslim quarter where the explorer James Bruce first stayed. The minaret of a mosque rises from a dense pack of tin roofs. We'll look at that later but first we head east to get a better sense of its position on the battlefield on Nov. 27, 1941.

---

[59] Mark Pilkington *Some Letters 1939-1942*, p. 205.

We come out on Gondar's eastern edge. In front of us is a valley of fields, parched yellow by the dry season, with a ribbon of green running through them. It marks where the Angereb River flows. Beyond the river on the left I recognize Defecha Ridge. I point out to Mulatu where we found the remains of the Italian stone fortress, almost hidden behind the band of eucalyptus trees at its south end. The one that was pounded by the guns of my father and the 54th Nyasaland Field Battery. Mulatu asks a group of boys, who take a break from their street soccer to watch us, what the ridge to the right and in front of us is called. There's a moment of silence while they peer over their shoulders. "Maldiba" one of them shouts. Maldiba Ridge was the 54th Nyasaland's last target. Where they concentrated their fire once Defecha Ridge had been taken. 4/4 KAR, a Ugandan infantry battalion, took it easily and with few casualties, unlike the bloody fight for Defecha.

From Maldiba we look for a group of ridges further to the south. That's where the Patriot forces including Pilkington and the Wollo Banda were positioned, in the two-mile gap between the British forces deployed to the east of Gondar, including Ayba Ridge where the 54th Nyasaland had its guns, and those to the south under the command of Brigadier J. James.[60]

On November 26, the eve of the battle, Pilkington, his liaison officer Molloy and his fellow British Patriot commander, Neil McLean, crouched on a hilltop beyond another river, the Megach. Like Pilkington, McLean originally fought with Wingate and had been in the Gondar area for several months. They surveyed the Italian strongpoints they were to attack in the morning known as the Fantar forts. McLean had earlier drawn a detailed map showing where each of the Italian forts were located. "We crossed the Megach River with the new moon," Pilkington writes, "and lay up that night in the scrub below the Fantar forts. I attacked before dawn, and by 8 o'clock we had stormed and taken all four forts. The Blackshirts Fascist militia fought well here, and were mostly killed."[61]

"Those forts would have been on some ridges just this side of where the Megach River flows," says Mulatu, pointing south beyond Maldiba Ridge. "Close to where

---

[60] David Shirreff, 'Bare Feet and Bandoliers,' p. 268.

[61] Mark Pilkington, *Some Letters 1939-1942*, p. 153.

the dam for a new reservoir is being built." After taking the Fantar forts, Pilkington radioed Molloy their next shocking move. "Bill McLean and his Eritrean battalion on my left flank, pushed on towards Azezo," he later wrote. "I decided to go for Gondar itself. We had to take the very high ground on each side of the valley leading up to the town. We had big Italian 104-mm guns on to us, and ran into our own Air, which was trying to help the regulars of 25th Brigade."

Braving shell bursts and strafing from RAF and South African pilots, who were supporting the attack and mistook them for retreating Italian forces, the Wollo Banda forged ahead. Molloy who at first was afraid to report what was going on now broke radio silence, "At 1400 hours I could contain my joy and excitement no longer and signaled Brigade HQ, "Shells bursting on old road to Gondar, Mark Pilkington beating Brigadier to it." He was referring to Brig. James whose 25th KAR Brigade was moving more slowly further south towards Azezo with support from Yeatman's Kenya armored car unit.

The Wollo Banda's new objective was the Italian cavalry station at Addis Alem. We get back in our *bajajs* and head back into the Muslim quarter whose edge we saw earlier. Nasi had already committed his crack reserve unit, the 22nd Brigade under Col. Torelli, to oppose what he saw as the main threat in the South, the 25th Brigade under Brigadier James. The Italian force defending Addis Alem was a much smaller and less formidable one. It was soon overwhelmed by the hard-charging Wollo Banda. As we drive along the bustling main thoroughfare of Addis Alem, Mulatu shares his theory on why the Wollo Banda were the first to reach Nasi. "They weren't from here, Wollo is the next region to the east, but I believe they quickly attracted support from local Patriots in Gondar itself. So, their numbers swelled, and the local Patriots also showed them the quickest route into the city."

At the bridge over the Qaha River which cuts through Addis Alem we pause. "This is the route they would most likely have taken, along the banks, and then pfft — ," he makes the sound through his lips followed by a sharp gesture with one arm, "up through the low point at Basha Sherif and on through the Saturday Market, where we turned, and up to Fasil Ghebbi." It seems logical but is there any historical proof to support it? That's a task for another day.

DAY SEVEN — Sunday, 3/19/23

Over breakfast at the hotel, I meet up with Girma Tayachew. He's a historian at the University of Gondar I've been introduced to by Haile Larebo, the professor at Morehouse in Atlanta. I'm hoping he will be able to help determine if Mulatu's theory is correct about how Pilkington and the Wollo Banda fought their way so boldly and unexpectedly all the way to Nasi's headquarters in the Town Hall next the Castle Enclosure. Girma is burly for an academic, pugnacious and at the same time humorous. Initially we seem to get into a sparring match over Gondar's World War II history. He's suspicious of British casualty figures being inflated, saying he's had trouble finding records confirming more than just a small handful of their troops being killed. Behind it I sense he's intimating that, as a foreigner, I shouldn't presume to know all the facts about Ethiopian World War II history. So trying a different tack, I tell him what I'm really eager to learn more about is the role the Patriot forces played, particularly in the final capture of Gondar. Girma's attitude changes immediately. He says Gondere Bagashaw, which literally translates to "Gondarees in the Shield," is the definitive account of the Patriot war in this area. It's written by Gerima Taferes, an important playwright and historian from that time. He's the father of Haile Gerima, a well-known Ethiopian filmmaker based in the United States. I ask if he has a copy, or better yet, if he does, would he bring it and come with me to Kulqualber, the narrow mountain pass controlling access from the South and scene of a crucial battle leading up to the final assault on Gondar, where the Wollo Banda Patriots under Pilkington first proved what extraordinarily brave fighters they were. He agrees and we set a date for Tuesday.

By late morning the search team and I are back in a pair of *bajajs* setting off on a quest that I hope will finally reveal the location of 54th Nyasaland's fourth and most challenging target — the elusive Dunquam Hill. Mulatu and I once again share the same *bajaj*. Since his original hunch that it was just a linguistic mix up, Dunquam substituted for Qusquam, didn't pan out, he seems equally eager to find out if this really is the place where General Nasi moved one of his heavy artillery units on the eve of the battle. [62]

At the north end of town, we stop to pick up our go-to guards, Alemu and Yohannes, who each squeeze into one of the *bajajs*. Maybe because he's ditched his uniform in favor of civilian clothes and seems unusually talkative today, I don't even recognize that it's Yohannes traveling with us at first. He laughs when I tell him and says through Mulatu "It's Sunday, time to relax." Ahead of us the lead *bajaj* waits for a break in the oncoming traffic and then turns off onto a side road. We follow and begin climbing a steep tree-covered hill. Kebrom was right, it's paved, but with the old-style cobbles we've seen elsewhere in Gondar. After riding up the bumpy incline for no more than a mile or so the road levels out and becomes a dirt track crossing some rolling fields. But as we saw on the way to Ayba, these vehicles are extremely versatile and can cope with almost any type of terrain. Soon we pull up behind Kebrom and Scott in a grassy space next to Gonderoch Giorgis church.

Sunday service is just over. The village priest and some of his congregation are gathered in the shade of a tree across from the church. In his white wrap and turban, the priest walks over to meet us. His name is Gebremariam. Kebrom explains who we are and why we're here. Among the first few words that come out of Gebremariam's mouth, I distinctly hear it — "Dunquam." I shoot a glance at Mulatu who nods and smiles. So this IS the place I'm looking for. As he speaks the priest indicates several high points around us. When Kebrom translates it turns out that the Italians built forts on two different hills.

Before we can begin exploring them though we're first invited inside the parish hall. It's a traditional building whose walls are made of thin wooden eucalyptus poles covered with mud and straw. As we learned yesterday from Mulatu the Lenten fast is suspended on weekends, so the villagers are enjoying a communal lunch together, with women and children sitting on one side, men on the other. Taking our seats along the back mud-stuccoed wall, we're offered shiny metal cups which are soon filled with a brown liquid called *tela*. It's an alcoholic drink made from barley and buckthorn berries, another Lent tradition. The server with a twinkle in

---

[62] Angelo Del Boca, 'Gli Italiani in Africa Orientale Vol. 3 La caduta dell' impero,' 1982, p. 526.

his eye encourages us to drink as much as we want. Get hammered and then go hiking in the afternoon heat? Not a choice I'm anxious to make. Fortunately, Ethiopians aren't strict enforcers of their traditions, so we get by with a few sips. It has an interesting taste but not enough to make me or Scott want more to fortify us for what's ahead.

When the meal is over, we say goodbye and Alemu as usual leads the way. Dunquam or rather Dunquan, as Mulatu says it should be correctly spelled, means 'tent' in Amharic. Perhaps it refers to the shape of the hill that looms above us as we leave a narrow, cultivated patch next to the village. From here the going gets tough. I find myself grabbing on to bushes to haul myself up through loose stones and soil as we head straight up. Then Alemu finds a footpath that goes more diagonally up the slope. After zigzagging back and forth a couple of times we come out on a crest where a herd of cattle are browsing among the dry brush. We pause for a minute to catch our breath and look back at the village below us. Kebrom points to the power lines which pass to one side of it. The priest was telling him over drinking *tela* that the village hadn't been hooked up to them yet and did he know anyone who could help. One of Kebrom's strengths, I'm discovering, is his extensive network of connections. He told the priest he knows someone who works at the local office of the World Bank and promised he would speak to him about the village's need for electricity. "Maybe it will lead to some action," he says.

As we continue to climb, the path leads us straight through the herd of browsing cattle. This time I'm bringing up the rear. Evidently, I get too close to one of the cows, spooking her. Immediately the hump-backed bull turns and takes a few threatening steps towards me, fixing me with a dark-eyed stare under his lowered, pointed horns. Instinctively I freeze, looking out of the corner of my eye for the best escape route. After what seems like a long time he turns and follows the cow. I join the rest of the group who have been smirking and stifling chuckles at my predicament. Scott tells me he took the perfect photograph. The caption would read "Man about to be gored by bull in search for lost World War II battlefield."

Alemu now leads us across a ploughed field full of large rocks. The far side is fringed with eucalyptus trees, a promising sight. From Google Earth I remember that the hill overlooking Gonderoch Giorgis is crowned with forest. Soon we're inside the trees and following a path. Then Alemu spots something and veers off to the right. And there it is, the remains of a circular stone fort made of black basalt. After inspecting it briefly we continue forward looking for a vantage point. Any guns positioned here would need to have a clear shot at the British forces attacking from the east. Soon we find a break in the trees and in the distance, I can make out Defecha and Ayba Ridges. So, the location fits but one thing baffles me. General Nasi ordered 20 artillery pieces to be moved down from Ambazzo the day before the battle. Only how could his crews have hauled three of those heavy guns up here? There's no sign of any road or even track they could have used.

The priest spoke of several sites so we continue through the eucalyptus forest. Alemu has picked up the pace, moving with what seems like a growing sense of urgency so I decide to stick close to him. For no obvious reason that I can see he decides to start heading more to the left. The slope gets steeper, once again I'm grabbing on to the vegetation to haul myself up. We climb over what looks like just another pile of rocks and then suddenly I realize I'm standing on what is obviously an old roadbed. To the left it goes almost straight downhill through the forest while to the right it curves round a bend and on up. "Found the way the Italians brought their guns up!" I yell excitedly back to the others.

As the road reaches the crest of the hill, Yohannes suddenly darts off through the underbrush to the left and starts shouting for us to come and see what he's found. He's standing in what is clearly a trench with rock walls on either side. But the best is yet to come. 20 yards further up the road which has almost reached the peak of the hill is another trench. It runs parallel to the treeline and through it the view I've been expecting opens up. With my binoculars I search for that distinctive pink circle that has come to represent the center of the Gondar World War II universe. And there it is, the roof of Kidanemihret church on Defecha Ridge. From there the other landmarks fall into place — Debre Birhan Selassie church, Gantz Hill, Maldiba Ridge and of course the unmistakable Ayba Ridge, where the guns of 54th Nyasaland were dug in behind their sandbags. Around noon on Nov. 27, 1941, their gun crews received an urgent radio call from their forward observers, "Enemy guns beyond Gondar firing on forward infantry."[63] 2/2 KAR were getting shelled by 54th Nyasaland's fourth and most difficult target. Quickly they sighted their guns on this spot almost 9 miles away, at the extreme edge of their range. It

---

[63] War Diary of 54th Nyasaland Field Battery Nov. 27, 1941, (See Appendix).

also meant they had little room for error. A fraction of a degree to the right or the left and they would miss their target entirely. When they'd dialed in the fresh co-ordinates the battery fired, reloaded and fired again, 19 high explosive shells went arcing through the air over Gondar. They landed right here. This is Dunquan Hill!

The War Diary and the words scribbled on the 54th artillery map itself euphemistically record what happened — "guns engaged and silenced." Standing now some 80 years later on the very spot, I struggle to grasp what that meant. Did the first few shells land nearby, giving the Italian gunners a chance to run for cover and save themselves? Or did those shells score a direct hit? A direct hit by a 25-pound high explosive shell would destroy a gun and tear its crew into body parts. Finally identifying this battle-scarred place, now returned to a peaceful forest, is exhilarating but at the same time horrifying. I'm suddenly brought face to face with the stark reality of war, a war in which my father was an active participant. Spurred on most likely by one thought — whether you're a gunner or a frontline infantryman it's still kill or be killed. Italian losses were high in the final battle — some 1,750 troops from national and colonial battalions.[64]

The rest of the group have already started back down the hill. But I remain rooted to the spot, trying to process thoughts and emotions stronger than any I experienced up on Ayba Ridge, that men could have died right here, killed by a shell fired by my father and his gun crew. When the others are almost out of sight I follow. Alemu is picking his way down the backside of Dunquan Hill. The route takes us through some steep cultivated fields. Then, as we move into a flatter area, the dry brush ahead parts to reveal the remains of a third stone fort. As Scott and I begin examining what's left of a curved wall, out of the corner of my eye I catch sight of a bizarre apparition — a monk dressed in a black hat and pale-yellow robe, clasping his hands above a large wooden cross, is standing at the opposite of end of the fort. A man of peace suddenly materialized into a theater of war. My Ethiopian companions at first seem equally stunned by his unexpected appearance, but then we find out that, standing outside his nearby monastery, he could hear us passing by and was curious to see who we were. The monk leads us back and down

---

[64] Angelo Del Boca, 'Gli Italiani in Africa Orientale Vol. 3 La caduta dell' impero, 1982, p. 529.

to his modest living quarters above a church that is visible through the trees. The order is dedicated to Saint Yared, a 6th century Ethiopian monk. He was poor and uneducated in his youth, until one day he saw a tiny caterpillar gamely climbing up the trunk of a tall tree to feed on its leaves.[65] It inspired him to overcome his lowly position and become a musician and composer of church music. Yared monastery surprisingly has both monks and nuns. They seem pleased to see us, glad of some guests with whom they can share the weekend break in their Lent fast. A nun in a bright orange robe offers us green mugs and more *tela*, the alcohol drunk at Lent we sampled earlier. This time I'm happy to join the celebration. Finding the elusive fourth target of the 54th Nyasaland Field Battery feels like another major accomplishment. After toasting our success and our monastic hosts we bid them farewell. We continue down through the trees until after a few minutes we strike part of the road we came up. As if by magic the two *bajajs* that brought us are waiting to take us back to Gondar, summoned by Kebrom on his phone.

The terrace of the Gondar Plaza Hotel is already a hopping place when we arrive back. Students from the University of Gondar campus up the road are returning to begin a new semester. Many are enjoying food and drinks in the soft evening light. Scott and I quickly snag a free table. Over an especially delicious fish goulash and beers we recall some of the extraordinary moments of the past week. Tomorrow Scott is leaving, off to Lalibela, famous for its rock hewn churches. It's also the place where Haile Selassie spent two days in prayer after losing the decisive battle of Mai Chew against the Italians on March 31st, 1936.[66] A month later he was forced to flee the country. The church in Lalibela where he spent his time praying was Bet Medhane Alem, said to be carved in the same shape as the church that originally held the Ark of the Covenant in Axum.

Somehow our conversation pivots to a critical moment in the history of ancient Greece. With tyranny, debt, and slavery threatening to undermine democracy in Athens, Scott tells me, the philosopher, Solon, turned to the Cretan shaman, Epimenides, for some wisdom and advice. Inspired by what he heard, Solon was

---

[65] Charles L. Chavis, 'Biography of St. Yared' on Black Past https://www.blackpast.org/global-african-history/saint-yared-505-571/

[66] Jeff Pierce, 'Prevail: The Inspiring Story of Ethiopia's Victory over Mussolini's Invasion,' Ch. 15, A King's Lonely Prayer, pp. 296-306.

able to introduce reforms which averted disaster and restored democracy. The defeat of the Italian invaders in Gondar, thereby liberating the whole country for the first time in five years, must have unleashed a similar wave of euphoria here and across the rest of Ethiopia.

Meeting up with Mulatu Wubneh & Kebrom Tekle

Gondar main square with Emperor Tewodros statue

Visiting Fasilides Castle

Scott Engel & guide Abebe Abiye at Qusquam palace

Casket with Empress Mentewab's skeleton

Meeting Feleke, Patriot fighter's son

Guard Alemu points to Ayba Ridge

Ruined Italian fort on Defecha Ridge

Abbot greeting us at Gorgora church

Boat ride on Lake Tana

Receiving blessing from 137 yr-old monk

Meeting with Ayba headman at 'Jambo Field'

Pointing to Gondar targets with Ayba villagers

Kebrom explains goal of my search

Wunania, same view photographed by my father

Battle of Gondar painting

Kids in front of Maldiba Ridge

Monk appears in Dunquam fort

54th NY Field Battery sergeants, Bruce Wickham, front row center

54th NY Field Battery truck on dusty road

54th NY Field Battery dug in on Ayba Ridge, Nov. 27, 1941

Ethiopian Highlands panorama

Wollo Banda Patriots commanded by Capt. Mark Pilkington
Source & Credit: Capt. Mark Pilkington

Gen. C.C. Fowkes Field HQ on Ayba escarpment
The National Army Museum, London

Gen. C.C. Fowkes Field HQ on Ayba escarpment
The National Army Museum, London

Crown Prince Asfaw Wossen giving victory speech from balcony of Fasilides Castle
The National Army Museum, London

DAY EIGHT — Monday, 3/20/23

Scott's departure the following day turns out to be a bumpy one. In the aftermath of the recent civil war between the Federal Government and the province of Tigray, tourists are still remarkably few in Ethiopia. During the time we've been staying in the Gondar we've seen only a handful in our hotel. A Chinese couple, and a solitary German are the only ones I can recall. But in the last few days an unusual group showed up. They consist of an Austrian couple who run an independent movie theater in the lake district outside Vienna, a blonde Slovenian woman and her extremely tall son who specialize in visiting out-of-the-way places. They're accompanied by an Ethiopian guide who they met in a province in the far south of the country which goes by a mouthful of a name — Southern Nations, Nationalities and Peoples. What's drawn them and Scott together is their shared desire to visit the fabled monolithic churches of Lalibela. They're literally carved out a single giant slab of often rose-colored rock.

On Mondays only, there's a direct flight from Gondar to Lalibela which this eclectic group is intending to catch. But the plan suddenly seems to go awry. At noon when the hotel shuttle bus is supposed to take them to the airport, neither the bus nor driver are anywhere in sight. When frantic phone calls fail to produce any result, Fasil, the hotel manager, runs out into the street and corrals three *bajajs*. Two of them leave, Scott and the Ethiopian guide in one of them. But the third that's supposed to take the Slovenian mother and her son is having a difficult time. His huge frame and equally large backpack refuse to fit inside the cramped inner quarters of the *bajaj*. Eventually, with backpack wedged precariously forward into the driver's space, they're able to set off. Scott would message me later that his ride ran into another nail-biting delay, it had to stop en route for gas but somehow, they did make the flight.

My day thankfully proceeds at a more leisurely pace. At 2 PM in the hotel lounge I meet with Bitwoded Dagnew, the academic we'd met at the Mandabba monastery on Lake Tana. Yesterday's momentous discovery of Dunquan Hill and the events that took place there are still reverberating in my mind. But it's a relief to escape from them at least temporarily. And, as I've already discovered, what makes Ethiopia such a fascinating place is how easily the present can suddenly and unexpectedly slip into the past. It's as if the two are constantly communicating with one another.

Bitwoded explains that the focus of his doctoral thesis is the relations between four monasteries during Gondar's golden age in the seventeenth and eighteenth centuries, as well as their complicated relationship with the Jesuits. Since we only had time to visit the north end of Lake Tana around Gorgora, he shows me photos of some treasures held at Daga Estifanos, an island monastery at the south end of the lake. They're not of rare, illuminated scrolls or manuscripts this time but the mummified remains of some of Gondar's most famous emperors — Susenyos and Fasilides among them. Iyasu the Great, who reigned after them, is buried on Mitraha, another island off the northeast shore. James Bruce recounts being shown his grave there.[67] Impatient to become emperor himself, Iyasu's son, Tekle Haymanot, had him murdered. This action inaugurates the beginning of *Zemena Mesafint* — the Era of the Princes. The time when Ethiopia's emperors became figureheads rather than the true wielders of power.[68] That fell to the likes Ras Mikael Sehul, the Tigrayan prince, who as a favor made James Bruce an honorary commander of the imperial cavalry. As Bitwoded tells me now, Ras Mikael also gave James Bruce a number of Ethiopian manuscripts, among which may well have been a copy of the Book of Enoch. I said my friend Scott would be intrigued to hear that. Ras Mikael probably saw it as yet another way to express his gratitude to Bruce for curing his son of smallpox.

But what intrigues me most is what Bitwoded has to say about the second aspect of his thesis, the relationship between the monasteries — and therefore Ethiopian Orthodox Church itself — and the Jesuit Order.

---

[67] James Bruce 'Travels to Discover the Source of the Nile'(1790 edition), Vol. 2 Book 4, pp. 515-516.

[68] Harold G. Marcus, 'A History of Ethiopia,' The decline of the Solomonic dynasty, pp. 44-46.

In 1603, when the Jesuit priest Pedro Paez arrives, Ethiopia is at a critical moment. Susenyos is about to become emperor. He has already seen how Portuguese soldiers and their muskets have helped Ethiopia reinvigorate itself militarily. Now he wonders, can Europe also help reinvigorate the country spiritually? Under Pedro Paez's guidance and advice Susenyos first converts to Roman Catholicism in secret. Then, in 1621, he goes public, proclaiming that Catholicism will replace the Ethiopian Orthodox Church as the official religion. But just as Susenyos begins his conversion campaign in earnest his most crucial ally, Pedro Paez, dies and is replaced by a much more militant Jesuit priest, Afonso Mendes. Mendes' heavy-handed approach — mass baptisms, priests being forcibly re-ordained and churches reconsecrated — alienates the people and leads to violent uprisings which have to be quelled with military might. After a particularly bloody battle with thousands dead on both sides, a group of defeated peasants, "heretics" as Mendes called them, delivers a desperate plea to the emperor. "We are all rushing on a sure course toward death. Not one of those men, with whose bones the earth is filled, is a foreigner; not one of us here has not lost a brother, a son, or some other to whom we are bound by blood."[69] Shortly before his death and filled with remorse, Susenyos reinstates the Ethiopian Orthodox Church. But it is left to his son, Fasilides, to take the most decisive step of banishing the Jesuits from the empire.

To throw new light on this story what Bitwoded most urgently needs is a contact at the Vatican archives. He's discovered that a trove of key documents are held there, letters sent by Emperor Susenyos to Pope Leo XI and King Philip III of Spain. At the time these were arguably the two most powerful men in Europe, making the words that Susenyos addressed to them all the more critical for him to gain access to for his study. As he leaves, I promise Bitwoded that Scott and I will do whatever we can to help him.

After his departure, I go out onto the hotel terrace and find a table in the shade. Sitting and watching the bustling street below, I suddenly realize that Bitwoded and I face similar challenges in our different endeavors. Just as Susenyos' letters would give him a clearer understanding of the emperor's state of mind at a critical moment in Ethiopian history, a few letters or a diary in which my father described

---

[69] 'The Jesuits in Ethiopia, 1609-1641: Latin Letters in Translation,' 2017, Edited by Wendy Belcher, Chronology & Introduction by Leonardo Cohen, p. 14.

his wartime experience here in Gondar would have been immensely valuable to me. But since he left no such personal account, just a few photographs, to reconstruct his story from, I must rely on secondary sources like the 54th Nyasaland War Diary and Colonel Bingham's oral history. That and meticulously following writer Tony Horwitz's dictum — "half the research is going to where the history happened." In the seven days I've spent here so far, I've managed to track virtually every move my father and his gun battery made — go to Ayba where they fought, locate the targets they hit. Everywhere the landscape, the buildings and the people have yielded important clues to the puzzle. The only course open to me is to stick with the strategy.

Towards the end of the afternoon Kebrom arrives to meet me as planned. We need to go over the details of the following day's expedition, the last we'll be making out of the city. It's an hour south of Gondar at a place called Kulqualber which played a key role in the campaign to overcome General Nasi and his remaining Italian forces in the city and the Amhara region. We'll have Teddy, the same driver and his car who took us to Gorgora. I tell Kebrom, Girma Tayachew, the historian I met yesterday, is coming with us. He lives in Azezo, to the south, so we can pick him up on the way.

Afterwards he invites me to take a walk up the hill to see his business, a copying and scanning service strategically located opposite the entrance to the University of Gondar where his target market — college students — can easily find it. On our way, we pass a kiosk where a cluster of them are out in front. "I hope that's not a competitor," I say. Kebrom grins, "No they're just getting duplicate keys made for their rooms." As we continue walking, we arrive at Kebrom's shop. It's a modest affair, a poster showing a copier and someone scanning a document is displayed on the front wall. A makeshift awning made from a blue tarpaulin shades the entrance. Inside we meet his manager, a young woman. She says business has picked up a bit with the students coming back. But the place is empty right now. It's clear that for recent college graduates like Kebrom, Ethiopia is a hard place to make a living, let alone find meaningful work. So, finding a side gig, like organizing this expedition to track down my father's wartime movements, is something he's constantly on the lookout for.

That stirs in me an idea that I've been waiting for the right moment to put to him. Before I'd even set off for Ethiopia, I was keenly aware of the uncanny parallels that exist between 80 years ago and today. When my father arrived outside Gondar, Ethiopia was trying to end a war, one in which the Italian occupation had merged into the global conflict of World War II. Now the country is trying to end another struggle, this time a civil war pitting the Tigray region against the Federal Government. Gondar is part of the Amhara region which borders Tigray and there's a long history of rivalry between the two. Our guards, Alemu and Yohannes, dressed in camouflage and armed with their AK-47s — even though they carry them so casually I sometimes forget they're a lethal weapon — had immediately come to embody that eerie continuity of struggle between my father's war and theirs, in which the fighting ceased just a few months ago.

At the end of our first day's hike up Defecha Ridge, Alemu had told me he'd got his first rifle at 18. He'd carried one now almost every day for 30 years, it was a part of him. In the days that followed I learned through Kebrom that both he and Yohannes had taken part in the conflict with Tigray. What was that like I wondered and how had the experience affected them? With only a few days left I needed to find out. "I'd like to interview Alemu and Yohannes," I told Kebrom. "Can you see if they'd be willing to do it on Wednesday, my last day?" "Of course," he said, and went on to tell me a story Alemu had shared with him just yesterday up on the summit of Dunquan Hill, where the shells from the 54th Nyasaland had exploded on the Italian battery. "We were up here fighting for almost two years," Alemu told him, "And we lost three of our comrades." The parallels it seems weren't just in my mind, they were real.

DAY NINE — Tuesday, 3/21/24

We're off to another early start. Girma Tayachew, the historian who's coming with us today has to be back for a meeting in the early afternoon. So I'm already down in the hotel lobby waiting when I see Kebrom and his driver Teddy pull up in the street outside.

As we head south, I'm rehearsing in my mind the sequence of events that took place in the weeks leading up to the final assault on Gondar. The 54th Nyasaland Field Battery had arrived north of the city on November 16 and began firing at Nasi's northern defenses from Argiv Ridge the following day. Their action served two purposes. It was to get them familiar with their new 25-pounder guns they'd picked up just days before at the port of Massawa on the Red Sea. It was also intended to distract the Italian defenders from where the main attack was to be launched — from the East and the South. But to make that possible the British commander, General Fowkes, first had to dislodge the Italian garrison that still controlled a narrow mountain pass on the southern approach to Gondar, thus opening the way for badly needed reinforcements in the form of a heavy artillery battery and a squad of armored cars from Kenya.[70]

Soon we reach Azezo, the town immediately south of Gondar where the modern airport is located. It began as an airstrip built by the Italians. As I saw when I first arrived the overgrown concrete skeletons of a few of their buildings still stand at the north end of the runway. We turn left off the main road, making our way along a busy side street. A crowd is milling around market stalls on either side selling everything from produce to furniture. We pull up outside an apartment building. Kebrom calls Girma to let him know we're here. As promised, he arrives clasping his copy of Gondere Bagashaw, the Patriot history he told me about at our first meeting. Once we're back on the main road and heading south, Girma

---

[70] Lt. Col. Hubert Moyse-Bartlett, 'The King's African Rifles Vol. 2,' Ch. 21, p. 148/561.

starts to share some of the book's highlights. It gives the names of 1,300 Patriots who died fighting in Gondar and 3,000 more who died elsewhere in Ethiopia.

As Girma works his way through the book, summarizing different passages, it's clear to me it does provide a uniquely Ethiopian perspective on the Patriots' war, one I've not heard before. Beginning with Wingate, the maverick British commander picked to lead Gideon Force and the guerrilla campaign to return Haile Selassie to power and continuing all the way through to the capture of Gondar. I ask him to focus on the Gondar section covered in the final 30 pages. Key players and places get intriguing mention — the 2nd Ethiopian Battalion and Col. Benson seizing Jenda, Sgt. Morrow firing captured Italian guns, the two battles of Kulqualber where we're headed today and whose correct pronunciation I now valiantly manage to master much to Girma's delight. When I'd initially called it Kul-karber, he looked at me blankly and said, "I've never heard of such a place." The book also mentions Pilkington and the Wollo Banda, and most intriguingly and unexpectedly the British artillery at Ayba. But I'll need to put a translator to work to find out the details of the account and whether it confirms Mulatu's thesis about how local Patriots joined the Wollo Banda and showed them quickest route into the city.

I first came across the story of the Wollo Banda in a book by David Shirreff. Shirreff fought in Ethiopia as the young lieutenant commanding a KAR infantry platoon. How he got there again reminded me of my father. After officer training in Britain, he volunteered to go to Kenya where he developed a healthy respect for his African troops, particularly one veteran Somali sergeant named Cora. He describes one key experience in his oral history — which I also found at the Imperial War Museum.[71] When the platoon first came under Italian machine-gun fire, Shirreff froze for a moment and it was Cora who took charge, shouting *twende* which in Swahili means "let's go." Regaining his composure, Shirreff followed as his platoon charged ahead across a river and captured an Italian trench. That experience probably influenced Shirreff's decision to write "Bare Feet and Bandoliers" in which he charts the important and previously unacknowledged role played by Patriot Forces which culminates in the campaign to liberate Gondar. Mulatu,

---

[71] Alexander David Shirreff Oral History, Cat. No. 7470, Imperial War Museum, London. https://www.iwm.org.uk/collections/item/object/80007272

a man well-versed in how World War II affected his hometown, confessed he'd never even heard of the Wollo Banda and their pivotal contribution in the Gondar campaign until he too read Shirreff's book.

The Wollo Banda weren't a local resistance group as most Patriot fighters were. Originally, they and 79th Foot, a colonial battalion from Eritrea, were recruited by and fought for the Italians. General Nasi, to express his high regard for colonial forces like these, said, "The Eritreans are famous, but for me the Ethiopians are also good."[72] When Nasi's garrison at Debre Tabor, a city southeast of Gondar, had surrendered in early July 1941, these two units were given the choice by the British to either switch sides or become prisoners of war. They chose the former. The Wollo Banda were placed under the command of Captain Mark Pilkington and the 79th Foot under Captain Neil McLean. Neither of these men were regular British officers. They'd fought for months as part of Col. Orde Wingate's successful guerrilla campaign.[73] Each commanded what Wingate called an Operational Center; a unit of one hundred well-trained Ethiopian troops armed with mortars and machine guns as well as rifles. These units attracted and led larger local Patriot forces in the fight that returned Haile Selassie to power. The Wollo Banda and the 79th now joined the ranks of Patriot fighters too as Pilkington and McLean pressed on towards Gondar.

Their new theater of operations became the countryside we're now driving through. It's flatter than the mountainous terrain we traveled through to the North of the city but still challenging. Just then I spot a volcanic plug rearing its grey head above the dun-colored fields on my left like some gigantic geological serpent. As we enter a rambling roadside village, Girma points to a turn-off on our left. "That's the road to Dogoma. The Italians originally had a fort there, but they were driven out by local resistance." Maybe it was Pilkington and the Wollo Banda. In August 1941 their first operation was to ambush an armed column of 58 trucks traveling down this road with supplies for the garrison at Kulqualber. The plan

---

[72] Angelo Del Boca, 'Gli Italiani in Africa Orientale, Vol. 3, La caduta dell' impero,' 1982, p. 508

[73] David Shirreff, 'Bare Feet and Bandoliers,' p. 232.

was to hit the column both coming and going. Pilkington describes what happened, "the Wollo were superb, chief honour must go to them." They destroyed 10 trucks, killing 6 officers and many native *askari* troops. Meanwhile McLean was harassing Italian movements to the South and East of Gondar. In the course of carrying out these guerrilla raids he drew detailed maps of the Italian defenses that proved invaluable to General Fowkes in planning his Gondar campaign. McLean also discovered the Ayba track that came to play such a vital part first at Kulqualber and then in the final attack on Gondar. The 54th Nyasaland War Diary even refers to the position they took up on Ayba ridge as the McLean's O.P. or Observation Post.

As we approach Kulqualber, the terrain changes drastically. Steep hills rise on either side of the road leaving only a narrow pass ahead. On the left a small flat area beneath a single large tree offers enough space for us to pull over. A family taking advantage of its shade studies us. An older woman clasps a large shiny silver platter in front of her. It's dented but delicately patterned.

Without guards for protection and someone who knows the way, Kebrom doesn't want us to risk climbing Kulqualber itself. Besides we're hardly equipped to take it on. The base is steep and rocky while the upper slopes seem to be covered with thick brush that would take a machete to cut our way through. But on the side of the pass where we're parked, a track leads up the hill. The British called it Pimple because of its shape. Nowadays its rounded peak is spiked with a tall communications tower of some kind. Kebrom, Girma, and I set off up the track. As we climb higher and look back it's easy to see why the British KAR forces and their Patriot allies had such a hard time attacking Kulqualber, its steep ridge extends like a natural battlement far to the west. At its far end, looking down on the shores of Lake Tana, were two other Italian fortified positions, Fercaber and Red Hill. The stronghold's commander, Col. Augusto Ugolini, was a veteran who'd been fighting in Ethiopia since the Italian invasion in 1935. With his 3,000 defenders he'd turned the whole ridge into a fortress capable of resisting attacks from both north and south. As one of his captains wrote "Against the English, against all of Ethiopia, my Italy alone I will I fight for you."[74] Girma suddenly beckons. On the

---

[74] Angelo Del Boca, 'Gli Italiani in Africa Orientale, Vol. 3, La caduta dell' impero,' 1982, p. 522.

south side of Pimple, he spotted some trenches hidden in the undergrowth beside the track.

Against these formidable defenses the first British attack on November 13th was poorly conceived and quickly failed. But by November 21st they had gained an important new advantage — the Ayba track discovered by McLean running to the east of Gondar. As Gen. Nasi later admitted, "my capital mistake was in not having foreseen that the track, which I also knew existed, could be rehabilitated and exploited to move forces between the two fronts of attack."[75] Coincidentally, his last remaining fighter aircraft, which could easily have spotted the British engineers at work and sounded the alarm, was also grounded for repairs at the time. As soon as his engineers had made the Ayba track passable to heavy vehicles, General Fowkes moved a whole brigade, the 25th infantry under Brigadier James, south thereby bypassing Gondar and reaching the very road we'd traveled down on. Once there the British regular troops were well positioned alongside the Wollo Banda to attack the Kulqualber and Fercaber fortresses from the North, while a second group of British and Patriot forces struck from the South.

In a report to his commander, Mark Pilkington describes the first hours of the attack, "There was no weak spot anywhere. I attacked Red Hill with four companies of Wollo. McDonald's Operation Center giving them covering fire with heavy machine guns and captured Italian mortars. The Wollo got close but were held up by those bloody bombs in trees which the Wops set off. Our mortars did good work on Red Hill but failed to silence the two cannons there, which shelled all approaches, firing at point blank range. The Wollo companies and McDonald's men withdrew a little and waited."[76] The 25th Brigade's KAR infantry also ran into dogged Italian resistance. After breaching the outer defenses, they were driven back in vicious hand-to-hand fighting by a ferocious Italian counterattack.

Meanwhile to the east of Pimple, the hill we've managed to climb up, the British assault from the south backed by other Patriot forces had stalled too. Capt. Peter Molloy, fighting his first action in this campaign, lay for hours next to a

---

[75] Angelo Del Boca, 'Gli Italiani in Africa Orientale, Vol. 3, La caduta dell' impero,' 1982, p. 524.

[76] Mark Pilkington, *Some Letters 1939-1942*, p. 148.

sapper or bomb disposal expert who'd been badly wounded by an Italian tree bomb like ones the Wollo ran into. Molloy remembers, "It was touch and go till 1430 hours when we overran the Italian Brigade HQ from several directions at once and the rest packed it in."[77] At the other end of the ridge, Pilkington's men seized their chance too, "the Red Hill garrison, seeing our people had not gone but were waiting with evil intent, and knocked about from the south by the heavy 60-pounder guns, lost their nerve and left their cannon position. The Wollo spotted the cannon was not firing and nipped in and the thing was over." Despite the stubborn fight put up by the veteran Italian garrison commander, Col. Ugolini — all three of his battalion commanders were killed and his casualties were a staggering 47 percent — the British attack succeeded this time.

But the Kulqualber victory came at a high cost for British and Patriot forces too. As Pilkington put it, "a shadow of gloom hangs over the picture in the shape of casualties. I do not know the total yet." When the numbers came in, he learned that the Wollo Banda suffered 55 dead, including several leaders killed by tree bombs, and 120 wounded. In spite of their high losses and unflagging fighting spirit, as Peter Molloy remembers, Brigadier James, the 25th Brigade commander, refused to be impressed, "It was a wonderful performance but being Patriots, they received little credit."

Although we aren't able to explore Kulqualber's main fortifications that proved so difficult for the British and Patriot forces to overrun, my experience at the other sites we've visited suggests they're most likely still there, preserved beneath the cloak of vegetation that covers the ridge. For an archaeologist studying World War II it would be an ideal site to investigate. Girma agrees and explains that the name Kulqualber in Amharic means "door of the cactus." It refers to a branching variety known as euphorbia which now seems to have disappeared. But just as we're about to leave Girma gives a shout and points. Sure enough, down on the edge of a plowed field and silhouetted against the ridge beyond is one lone, glorious survivor of the original cactus forest, a living memorial to the battle.

Our next stop promises to give me another deep dive into Gondar's and Ethiopia's history, in fact the deepest yet. But as we drive down the steep twisting stretch of road south of Kulqualber we suddenly come face to face with the natural

---

[77] Mark Pilkington, *Some Letters 1939-1942*, p. 202.

dangers that still lurk here even if it's no longer bristling with men and guns. Stretching almost across the entire road is a truck sprawled on its side, apparently caught off guard by a sudden hairpin bend. Carefully Teddy steers us around it.

Seeing the crashed truck reminds me of how the 54th Nyasaland Field Battery suffered its first and very high-profile casualty of the Gondar campaign. The Royal Artillery commander, Col. John Ormsby who'd worked so hard to get the battery ready in time for the Gondar campaign, was driving a jeep probably on this very road when he was hit by cannon fire from the last Italian fighter plane, now repaired and back in the air.[78] One of the bullets severed his femoral artery and he bled to death on the spot. But with the road through Kulqualber now open General Fowkes could bring in those reinforcements he so desperately needed including the Kenya armored car unit that will ultimately receive General Nasi's surrender.

The road south passes through Emfraz. Apart from one mosque with shining new minarets, there's nothing eye-catching about its dusty and dilapidated buildings that straggle along the side of the road. Evidently things have changed since the French explorer, Charles-Jacques Poncet visited in 1700. "The town is not so big as Gondar, but it is much more pleasant and in a finer situation. The houses themselves are better built. They are all separated from one another by quick hedges, always green and covered with flowers and fruit. The emperor's palace is seated up on an eminence, which commands the whole town."[79] It was also famous for the traffic of slaves and 'civet', a type of musk extracted from civet cats for use in perfumes. A hundred years later, Girma tells me, it became the birthplace of a famous woman, Emperor Tewodros's mother, Woizero Atitegeb Wondbewossen. Sometimes she was disparagingly called a *Kosso* meaning nothing but low-status "flower seller" because of the poverty in which she and her son were forced to live after she divorced his father.

Tewodros, as I'd learned by now, is regarded as one of Ethiopia's most prominent heroes. Gondar has two glittering golden statues to him. One on the main

---

[78] Lt-Col. Hubert Moyse-Bartlett, 'The King's African Rifles,' Vol. 2, Bartlett footnote, p. 143/556.

[79] Charles-Jacques Poncet, 'The Red Sea and Adjacent Countries at the close of the 17th Century,' edited by William Foster, The Hakluyt Society, 1949, p. 136.

central square, where with sword and shield he stands defiant against Mussolini's competing dream of an African empire expressed in the Italian buildings that still surround him. The other statue is in front of the airport where he strikes a similar pose. For putting an end to the chaotic and violent "Era of the Princes" that had persisted for a hundred years and reuniting the country, he's seen as the founder of modern Ethiopia.

Tewodros lacked a royal pedigree, at least one linking him directly the Solomonic imperial line. He lived as commoner but an astute and educated one. Originally named Kassa Hailu, he took the name Tewodros when he defeated his last rival and became emperor in 1855. It means Gift of God, thus cleverly aligning him with the prophecy that a king by that name would restore Ethiopia to greatness.[80]

He's also described as a *shifta* meaning an outlaw or bandit. It's how he learned and honed the military skills that enabled him to defeat all his princely rivals. Although in Tewodros' case, he was clearly an outlaw of the Robin Hood variety. He gave money to peasant farmers to buy ploughs and didn't shy away from hard labor himself, working at times alongside them in the fields. He unified Ethiopia and carried out much needed reforms, including a push to reduce slavery and improve the justice system. Surprisingly, given his high approval rating in Gondar today, he also burned the city. He moved his capital, taking with him the royal library of 1,000 scrolls, first to Debre Tabor and later to Maqdala, his mountain top fortress over two hundred miles to the east.

But Tewodros's determined and at times fanatical efforts to modernize his country and secure for his army the latest military technology ultimately bring about his downfall. Rather than spend their time saving souls he cajoles a handful of Protestant missionaries into to teaching Ethiopians the art of forging cannons. Those valiant efforts produce a huge mortar-like device, a model of which stands at the base of his statue in Gondar's main square. At the same time, he also sends letters to Queen Victoria imploring her to supply him with the military hardware he needs to defeat his arch enemy, "the Turk", as he refers to the Egyptians because of their Ottoman heritage, who now also control Ethiopia's neighbor, Sudan.[81] But with the American Civil War suddenly cutting off access to the world's main

---

[80] Bahru Zewde, 'A History of Modern Ethiopia, 1855-1991,' 2001, p. 28.

[81] Ibid., pp. 34-39.

cotton supply, Egypt's crop becomes essential to keep Liverpool and Manchester, the twin engines of Britain's Industrial Revolution, humming along. So, the British Government decides to ignore Tewodros's pleas.

When his letters go unanswered, Tewodros angrily imprisons the missionaries and several other British subjects. Britain in turn sends a military taskforce of 32,000 men and artillery under Sir Robert Napier to secure their release. Tewodros is besieged in his fortress at Maqdala. Two paintings at the Gondar airport immortalize the final act of the conflict. In the first Tewodros is on his favorite white horse next to the giant cannon, built with missionary help and named Sebastapol, as it's dragged into battle. But at the critical moment it fails to fire against the attacking British. In the second painting, as British troops charge towards him Tewodros raises a pistol to his mouth and commits suicide. The gun was in fact a gift from Queen Victoria. One of the macabre trophies brought back to Britain were the braids of Tewodros cut from his dead body. Only recently were they returned to Ethiopia.[82] The manner of his death has endowed Tewodros with the cult-like status of a Che Guevara or Bob Marley in Ethiopia. I'm not surprised by the way Kebrom describes him: "The right man at the wrong time." Because of that he remains a symbol of hope for Ethiopia's future.

A few miles beyond Emfraz we reach the turn off for Guzara palace, the one that Poncet had glimpsed "seated up on an eminence, which commands the whole town." Almost immediately I tell Teddy to stop a moment. I want to take a photo of the archetypal view I can see in front of us — a stone castle, perched up on a hill, with towers at its corners and walls glowing in the afternoon sun. As we drive on, the bumpy dirt road gets steeper, our wheels begin to spin. Teddy backs up and takes another run at it but with the same result. Time to get out and walk. With less weight on board Teddy can negotiate the rough spot and soon catches up with us. Why I've been curious to come here is that Guzara is considered the pre-cursor of the majestic imperial castles in Gondar.

We arrive at the outer stone wall surrounding the palace. The gate is locked but, following a path already worn by previous visitors, we grasp a conveniently overhanging tree branch and haul ourselves over the wall. As we approach the castle

---

[82] BBC News, 3/4/2019 'Ethiopian Emperor Tewodros II's stolen hair to be returned by UK.' https://www.bbc.com/news/world-africa-47441042

I can see it's undergone extensive restoration, fresh white mortar surrounds many of the stones. It's believed that Emperor Sarsa Dengel built Guzara around 1577 to celebrate his victory over the Ottoman Turks and later to push back incursions by the Oromo people from the south. As Girma tells me, others believe it was built earlier by Sarsa Dengel's uncle, Emperor Gelawdewos. With help from 200 Portuguese musketeers — the first Europeans to visit Ethiopia — he defeated and killed a very tenacious Muslim invader, Ahmad Gragn or Ahmad "the left-handed," in a battle fought somewhere near here, close Lake Tana. It's uncertain history and ruined state only make Guzara more intriguing. The ravens roosting on the battlements, which they seem to have adopted as their permanent home, bring to mind the ravens at the Tower of London. "What will happen to Ethiopia if they leave?" I ask Girma. He laughs and then says, "Maybe it means the emperor will return."

Whichever emperor built it, Guzara's battlements stand as a magnificent milestone, the earliest monument to a resurgent Ethiopian empire which peaked a century later in Gondar's urban splendor. First the emperors had repulsed the physical threat posed by the Muslim invader Ahmad Gragn, then they had forcibly rejected the spiritual threat they saw in Jesuit Catholicism. If Ethiopia faces a new existential threat they'll need a new champion. This is as good a place as any for that person to emerge. Looking up one last time at those stout stone walls I think of the British forces who passed by here on their way to Kulqualber. One soldier's account records that to take cover from the Italian guns ahead "on one patrol I lay in the doorway of an old Portuguese fort."[83]

On the drive back to Gondar the discussion switches from the struggles of the past to Ethiopia's present political situation. American Secretary of State Anthony Blinken has just paid a visit to Addis Ababa, his first since the ceasefire agreement signed between Tigray and the Federal Government. As Girma sees it, the message Blinken delivered to Prime Minister Abiy Ahmed was this: "Keep the peace or it will be the Amharas turn." Since the overthrow of the Derg in 1991, Ethiopia has been ruled by a system called Ethnic Federalism which strives to balance the interests of the country's different ethnic groups, the most dominant being the Tigrayans, the Amharas and the Oromo. The excesses of Tigrayan authoritarianism

---

[83] Michael Blundell, 'A Love Affair with the Sun: a Memoir of 70 Years in Kenya,' 1994, p. 64.

led to Abiy, an Oromo, coming to power. His early success was ending the twenty-year border war with neighboring Eritrea which brought him the Nobel Peace Prize. Then came the clash between Abiy and the Tigrayans that led to the civil war that's only recently ended. Will the peace hold? Can Abiy do a better job of performing the delicate balancing act between the ethnic groups? The jury is out but at least Ethiopians don't seem afraid to speak their minds. For Girma it means "Democracy hasn't been born yet in Ethiopia." For Kebrom: "Ethnic Federalism is the worst kind of federalism." In some ways these present concerns echo those earlier struggles that I've seen evidence of in the sites and situations I've encountered during my expedition to Gondar.

As we near the south end of the city we have to make a lengthy stop at a gas station to fill up. There's a long line of customers ahead of us. Looking through the window to my right I see on the other side of the road leading back into Gondar a sprawling construction site in a shallow riverbed. "What's going on there?" I ask. "That's the reservoir that Mulatu was telling you about the other day," Kebrom replies. Above the construction site I can see a ridge which would have held the first of the Italian Fantar forts. We're actually parked at the very spot that marks the southern front of the British battle lines drawn around Gondar.

According to General Fowkes' grand plan, while the 26th Infantry brigade, with artillery support from the guns of my father's 54th Nyasaland, were attacking Defecha and Maldiba Ridges on the eastern side, taking these Fantar forts was the objective he assigned to Pilkington's Wollo Banda and McLean's 79th Foot, the two Patriot forces who had demonstrated their fighting capabilities so impressively in the battle for Kulqualber. To the south of them, almost exactly at the gas station where we are, the other victors of Kulqualber, the 25th Brigade under Brigadier James, were given what was considered the primary objective of taking the airport at Azezo and the southern road leading into Gondar. But first they'd have to repair the bridge retreating Italian forces had destroyed across the very river I can now see being dammed.[84]

---

[84] David Shirreff, 'Bare Feet and Bandoliers,' p. 268.

DAY TEN — Wednesday 3/22/23

It's my last full day in Gondar. Fittingly perhaps I'm going to interview Alemu and Yohannes, the two guards who have come to represent an uncanny merging of past and present. Today I'm surprised to see them show up in civilian clothes. I've come to picture them always in camouflage uniform. But Alemu I notice is clasping his rifle clip in one hand as if it's a good luck charm. Later I'll discover it's because they've checked their rifles at the front desk. Yohannes is actually holding his claim ticket and will wave it constantly to illustrate what he's saying. We take them up to the lounge of the Gondar Plaza Hotel and settle in a corner around the same table where I first pulled out my father's artillery map to plot our objectives. The setting seems oddly formal after all the wild battle zones we've visited but it's quiet which is important since I want to record what they have to say.

I've written out about a dozen questions for Kebrom to ask. Of course, it would be best if he could translate their answers as we go, but I'm afraid that would take too long and interrupt the flow. So we've agreed he should work his way straight through, writing a summary of each answer as we go which he can then go over and translate for me afterwards. I set my phone to record and Kebrom begins. Unexpectedly Yohannes speaks up first. Out in the field he always seemed the more reticent of the two. He and then Alemu proceed to describe their militia unit.

"We're part of the Gondar City Administration Militia Office. We and our 85 colleagues can be called out day or night to perform peacekeeping and law enforcements duties." I'm surprised the unit is so small. I'd assumed it would consist of several hundred men at least.

"In November 2020 when the war in Tigray started, we were called up to the Chew Ber front, that's on the border between Amhara and Tigray, at a place called Adi Arkay, about 180 km from Gondar." They'd traveled along the very same road but in the opposite direction that my father's artillery unit took in November 1941, bringing their guns to attack Gondar. At Adi Arkay Alemu and Yohannes fought alongside the Ethiopian army, known as the Ethiopian National Defense Force, and a Special Regional Force, a reference to the main Amhara militia. The combined group quickly drove back the forces of the Tigrayan People's Liberation Front and within two weeks Federal troops occupied Mekele, the Tigrayan capital. By the end of the month Alemu and Yohannes were back in Gondar. "But several of our comrades didn't make it home and we miss them."

The following year in June, when the TPLF forces made a stunning comeback, retaking Mekele and pushing rapidly south towards Addis Ababa, Alemu and Yohannes were recalled to action, this time deploying to Debre Tabor and the Gashena Front close to the eastern border of the Amhara region. By December 2021 Federal troops and allied militias, including theirs from Gondar, had again driven the TPLF back into Tigray.[85]

But when I ask Alemu and Yohannes where they'd faced the greatest danger, they give a surprising answer. It was December 2020, on Defecha Ridge, the place we'd visited on our very first hike together. The day we'd looked for and found the Italian fort that the 54th Nyasaland Field Battery had pounded with 76 high explosive shells. "It was an unforgettable incident. We lost nine of our comrades and some the farmers fighting with us." It happened around the 'bastion,' the area with the first stone fort we encountered hidden in the dense brush. I remembered how quickly Alemu had wanted to move on after pointing it out and now I could understand why. It must have brought back painful memories of comrades killed. The action was against the same group that I was about to hear more about when Kebrom asks my next question: "What was the incident that brought you to Dunquan Hill before we went there?"

In May 2021 the Gondar City Militia Office deployed Alemu and Yohannes' group to the area around the Gonderoch Giorgis church where we'd located the Italian artillery position that the 54th Nyasaland Field Battery had put out of action. "We were deployed there for almost two years on and off. We made a rock shelter where we could take cover." The group they were fighting belonged to an

---

[85] Reuters, 12/11/21, 'As government offensive pushes forward, scars of war dot Ethiopia's Amhara region.' https://www.reuters.com/world/africa/government-offensive-pushes-forward-scars-war-dot-ethiopias-amhara-region-2021-12-10/

ethnic group known as the Qemant who it was believed were receiving arms and support from the TPLF in neighboring Tigray. The Qemant have lived in the Amhara region for centuries, perhaps longer. They have their own culture, religion and even language although it's fast dying out. During World War II, they had sometimes launched attacks against the local Patriot forces believing that the Italian occupiers were more likely to recognize and respect their separate culture and identity.[86] The same struggle for recognition and autonomy motivated their latest attacks in the area around Dunquan Hill.

The rock shelter Alemu, Yohannes and their comrades had used for protection was in fact the third and last Italian fort we'd found where the monk had suddenly surprised us. The operation they conducted "required more than 85 men and was ultimately successful." There's now a peace agreement in effect with the Qemant. "But we had to bury three of our friends up there next to the Yared monastery church. So, when we went there again with you, we naturally thought of our dead colleagues and how lucky we were to be alive."

One of the reasons Kebrom had selected Alemu and Yohannes to act as our guards was their extensive knowledge of the countryside around Gondar. It would help us find the World War II sites I'd come to explore. But I never imagined they themselves had fought in military actions similar to the ones that my father and his battery were engaged in during the battle to liberate Gondar, and that two of those actions were fought on the very same ground. They may not have been firing 25-pound explosive shells, but they were still fighting a war and seeing fellow soldiers die. For Alemu in particular, now in his late 40s, war seems to have defined his life, etching memories in the lines of his face. At 18 he joined the Ethiopian National Defense Force and fought in the long war against Eritrea. An exploding grenade severely wounded him in the chest, forcing him to take early retirement. But once he'd recovered, he decided to join the peacekeeping force in Gondar. He is a born soldier and firmly believes the cause he is defending is the right one. No wonder he clutched his rifle clip like a talisman as he told me about his experiences.

After saying goodbye to Alemu and Yohannes, Kebrom and I set off by *bajaj* on my last visit to the city center. Our first stop is the Ethiopian Airlines office for me to check in for my flight out the following day. It's located right next to the

---

[86] David Shirreff, 'Bare Feet and Bandoliers,' p. 235.

old Italian cinema with its curved yellow facade. Originally those newsreels I'd found would have been shown here. The ones that celebrated the Italian occupation and the ambitious building program already in progress that was going to transform Gondar into a "Second Rome".

One newsreel it certainly didn't show, unless under hastily established new management, was the one produced by British Movietone News to celebrate the liberation of Gondar. It shows the December 2nd, 1941, victory parade with General Wetherall, the British Commander-in-chief, inspecting, as the narrator tells us, "A brigade representative of all units engaged in the defeat of those last remnants of the Italian army which had held out in the region of Gondar." The first to pass in front of the general are the nine cars of the Kenya Armored Regiment, presumably to honor their commander Major Yeatman who received General Nasi's sword of surrender.[87] But they aren't followed by Captain Pilkington and the Patriots of the Wollo Banda who led the final and decisive charge into the city. Instead, a Scottish regiment in kilts, the Argyll and Sutherland Highlanders, led by their bagpipe band, is the next to march colorfully but undeservedly in front of the reviewing stand. Those same two images — the armored cars and the Scottish tartan caps — feature prominently in the Ethiopian painting of the battle of Gondar I'd seen in Ras Ghimb Museum. This newsreel, I presume, must be the source the painter was following.

But the Wollo Banda weren't to be denied. They held a victory parade of their own. On the morning of November 28, the day after Gen. Nasi's surrender, as Peter Molloy, the liaison officer for the Patriot forces, was driving through the streets of Gondar he came across an astonishing sight. It was Capt. Mark Pilkington "solemnly riding into town, surrounded by his rascally staff, on a magnificent white stallion from Nasi's stable. He was as cool and detached as usual and even dammed me for scaring his horse with my car before he recognized me!"[88]

The Wollo Banda Patriot fighters weren't the only ones who missed out on the official victory parade captured on the newsreel film. Sergeant Bruce Wickham

---

[87] 'Abyssinia Cleaned Up,' British Movietone News, 1/1/1942. https://www.youtube.com/watch?v=uQbhsY5T7iQ

[88] Mark Pilkington, *Some Letters 1939-1942*, p. 205.

and the 54th Nyasaland Field Battery didn't play any part in it either. With the capture of both Defecha and Maldiba ridges and General Nasi's surrender at the Town Hall in the late afternoon of Nov. 27, 1941, the 54th Nyasaland's job at Ayba was done. And it was done without a single enemy shell striking their position. After one more night in their tents at Jambo Field, the site the village priest had shown me, they hitched their guns back to their tow-trucks and traveled halfway back along the Ayba track to a point marked O.P. 3 on the artillery map.[89] Most likely it was where our 4-wheel drive vehicle had traveled along the very edge of the escarpment and a panoramic view of the valley and mountains had opened up next to us. From that position the battery could train their guns on the few Italian artillery positions still holding out on several peaks overlooking Gondar's northern access road. But the order to fire never came. As the War Diary records, on Nov. 29 "During the morning white flags seen on Deva and Ambazzo." Deva Ridge, although we couldn't visit it, was where the Italian crews after firing several volleys had pulled their guns back into the shelter of some caves, preventing the 54th from scoring a decisive hit when they returned fire.

By December 1st the 300 men of the 54th Nyasaland were back at a campsite close to the one they'd occupied when they first arrived just over two weeks before at Km 497 on the Gondar road. The nights, as the War Diary reports, turned "bitterly cold but the men seemed to stand up to them extraordinarily well." There they carried out repairs and continued training exercises. Not until December 7th did the men of the artillery battery that had been specifically raised for this campaign finally have the chance to see the city they'd helped liberate. It was a Sunday and the War Diary records they were to attend "Church parade. Parties of all denominations go to Gondar for divine service."[90]

As Kebrom and I walk out of the Ethiopian Airlines office and stand for a moment on Gondar's main square, the stone walls of the Castle Enclosure at one end and Emperor Tewodros' gleaming gold statue at the other, I can't help wondering if this is where my father and his fellow gunners in 54th Nyasaland arrived in their trucks on December 7th 1941, the same day that Japanese aircraft carrier planes attacked Pearl Harbor bringing the United States into World War II? Did

---

[89] War Diary of 54th Nyasaland Field Battery Nov. 28, 1941, (See Appendix).

[90] Ibid., Dec. 7, 1941, (See Appendix).

a young man of 24 who'd only been in Africa a few months, and in a place totally unlike this one, suddenly find himself standing open-mouthed in awe at the soaring towers and intricate stonework of the imperial palaces? Where was the "divine service" that he attended held? Was he surrounded by the colorful murals of Ethiopian saints at Debre Birhan church? And how did he feel about what he and his fellow soldiers — a handful of Europeans like himself, but mostly Africans from a country far to the south — had accomplished, finally freeing the one country in Africa which had remained free for virtually all of its 3,000-year history? Since he never talked about it, there's no way of answering these questions. And perhaps it's better that way. It leaves room for magical realism to supply the answers in a country where men can fashion rafts out of surfboard-shaped boulders and a swarm of bees can drive away an enemy about to set fire to an ancient place of worship.

By the time we get back to the hotel it's late afternoon. There's one more place I want to visit, the nearby hill on which the University of Gondar's southern campus sits. At its imposing entrance gate with its sweeping yellow arches and stonework we're asked to show ID. Kebrom talks in hushed tones to the security guard. He listens, nods several times and then waves us through. "What did you tell him?" I ask. "That we have an appointment with an important senior professor," he replies with a sly grin. Which of course we do, because we're going to meet up with Mulatu at the end of his day. But first we need to walk to the top of the hill. I want to check out one final hunch, a response in fact to Mulatu's constant advice to "keep digging." Looking at the Artillery map again I realized it shows the area where my hotel now stands, close to a place called Samunabar Saddle. When I mentioned it to Mulatu, he said "Yes, *samuna* means soap in Amharic. It was named after an old soap factory on the Azezo road, near the base of the hill on which the Gondar University campus was built." Drawn in red crayon along the crown of that hill, the Artillery map shows two squares. Inside one of them I can read the word "fort." These were Italian forts, or more accurately artillery positions up on the high ground where the university now stands.

Kebrom and I begin climbing the hill beyond the main gate. The road is steep, we pass students hurrying in the opposite direction, on their way either to their dorms or their next class. Established after the war, the campus is very much a place that's focused on Gondar's present and future, with its schools of business, law, social and environmental sciences. But it's also a place where history is respected and studied by scholars like Bitwoded and Girma who I had been lucky to meet.

Like the rest of the city the campus grounds are yellow and parched, thirsty for the first rains that are still more than a month away. We come to a traffic circle whose curbstones are painted in patriotic yellow, green and red and a single exotic pine stands in its center, leaning over to one side as if trying to reach some imaginary pool of water. After one more turn past the law school and Kebrom's old business classroom we reach the top of the hill. It's crowned with a half-completed open-air stadium. A crane arm hangs listlessly over it, waiting for more funding and supplies to finish the job. But what I'm interested in is the undeveloped patch of ground right in front of us. Covered in scrub and a few stunted trees and facing east it could well be the site of one of the two Italian heavy batteries marked on the artillery map.

I pull out my father's old binoculars. As expected, I can see off in the distance to the northeast the by now familiar ridges — Defecha and Maldiba. Beyond them the long hulking Ayba escarpment where the 54th Nyasaland unleashed its dawn bombardment. But what I'm curious about are the ridges further to the south. Like a camera, I pan my father's binoculars. There they are, three of them, nestled beside a curve made by the Megach River. That's where the Italian Fantar forts stood. And beyond them is where two units of Patriot Forces, the Wollo Banda and the 79th Foot were poised to attack. As Peter Molloy wrote, "the Wollo were first off the mark, moving amazingly fast in their bare feet."

Like the 54th Nyasaland Field Battery, neither the Wollo Banda nor any of the Patriot Forces were represented at the December 2nd 1941 victory parade held in nearby Azezo. Yet the Wollo Banda led by Capt. Mark Pilkington unquestionably struck the final blow in the liberation of Gondar. Drawing my gaze back I trace their line of attack, along the western flank of the Megach River. Today the valley is covered with a dense patchwork of mostly industrial buildings. But back then this was open country. The fighters of the Wollo Banda were running a deadly gauntlet, the most dangerous stretch of Pilkington's bold and improvised attack. They were dodging shells fired by 104mm guns, the heaviest the Italians had, mounted in the pair of forts up here where Kebrom and I are now standing. They also had to avoid machine-gun strafing from British planes swooping overhead and mistaking them for retreating Italian forces. Miraculously the Wollo Banda reached Addis Alem, the Muslim quarter we'd explored, and which lies below and in front of us. By then Pilkington and the Wollo Band had overcome the worst of the remaining Italian resistance and by 4pm they had cornered Gen. Nasi's in his last hideout, the Town Hall. Almost exactly a year later on November 18, 1942, Mark Pilkington was still fighting the Italians, now with Rommel's Afrika Korps in full retreat across Libya, their last remaining foothold in North Africa. Pilkington had joined the Long Range Desert Group, another British unit operating behind enemy lines. He was manning the machine gun mounted in the back of a jeep when he was hit and killed by bullets from an attacking Italian fighter plane.[91]

Kebrom points at his watch. "I think the Professor will have finished his class by now." We head back down, past the leaning tree and down the longest flight of steps I've seen in Gondar. At the bottom we run into Mulatu. Together the three of us walk down the street for a farewell drink on Plaza Hotel terrace. Four years in the making, delayed first by a pandemic and then by a war, my Gondar World War II expedition is drawing to a close. Mulatu asks me point blank, "So when can we see your account?" "Well, right now I don't have anything else on my plate," I confess. "But as you know there are a couple of loose ends to tie up with the story. For instance, what part did the local Patriots play? And did they assist the Wollo Banda? And for that I need Gerima Taferes' book "Gondere Bagashaw." Kebrom beams and reaching into his pack he pulls out a copy. "I found it in the bookstore."

---

[91] Christ Church College Oxford, Capt. Mark Leslie Pilkington. https://www.ch.ox.ac.uk/fallen-alumni/captain-mark-leslie-pilkington

Getting It Done — 6/24/23

Early one morning in November 1918, a haggard, sleep-deprived John Reed ran into his publisher, Max Eastman, on a New York street. He told him "I'm writing the Russian revolution in a book. I've got all the placards and papers up there in a little room and a Russian dictionary, and I'm working all day and all night. I haven't shut my eyes for thirty-six hours. I'll finish the whole thing in two weeks. And I've got a name for it too — *Ten Days that Shook the World.*" Then he hurried off to find some coffee. As Reed spoke what Eastman saw was "the unqualified, concentrated joy in his eyes. He was doing what he was made to do, writing a great book."[92]

***

My alarm goes off but it's already 7:30am. I realize I forgot to set it back an hour. I jump out of bed which surprises me. Usually, I have to do 20-30 minutes of stretches before I can move that quickly and easily. I text my friend Dave who I'm supposed to be meeting right now to go running with at the Carter Center. "Be there in 30 min."

I may not be in the same mad hurry as John Reed, but I've been writing steadily and there have been moments of "unqualified, concentrated joy."

It's three months since I got back from Ethiopia. If I hadn't been a runner I never would have had the stamina or physical fitness I needed to make the trip. But the one thing I never managed to do while I was there was go running in the land of Haile Gebreselassie and so many other elite long-distance runners. I imagined following a seven-mile circuit which would take me past the giant sycamore

---

[92] Max Eastman 'Heroes I Have Known: Twelve Who Lived Great Lives' p.223-24 & Wikipedia. https://en.wikipedia.org/wiki/Ten_Days_That_Shook_the_World#:~:text=He20%was%20gaunt%2C%20unshaven%2C%20greasy,Days%20that%20Shook%20the%20World!

tree at Jan Tekel where Emperor Fasilides first pitched his tent, then on through the main gate of the Castle Enclosure with its palaces, libraries, stables, steam baths and lion cages.

Today I'm going to run the closest equivalent I can think of here in Atlanta. Like Gondar, it's a city where a crucial battle was fought. I'm driving to the hill where on July 22nd 1864, General William Tecumseh Sherman established his headquarters as Union and Confederate armies clashed a mile to the South.[93] Today it's the home of the Carter Center, with its staunch commitment to conflict resolution, as well as improving global health and enhancing freedom and democracy. After parking my car, I can see Dave, my running partner, has already set off. I make my way past the vendors who are busy setting up booths for the Farmers' Market held in the parking lot here every Saturday. Coming out of the trees I cross to the footpath which runs alongside Freedom Parkway. That's the road that was built when the city came to its senses in the 1980s and in place of a neighborhood-destroying freeway built a more modest parkway thereby preserving much of the surrounding green space for trails like the one I'm now running on.

After a mile and a half, I turn onto the road that takes me down towards the epicenter of Atlanta's Civil Rights struggle, Ebenezer Baptist Church and the King Center where Martin Luther King is buried. Outside Ebenezer there's an enlarged photo of MLK and someone who at first glance looks like Malcolm X. The caption underneath is a quote from King. Words to the effect that Sunday School taught him a valuable lesson — how to "build the capacity for getting along with people."

Why I like to run is it gives me clarity. It helps me see a way forward when things are hard. In this case how should I end this account about a journey that took me to Ethiopia and back to Africa?

***

---

[93] 'The Civil War: Atlanta and Copenhill' James A. Yancey Jr. Former Archivist, Jimmy Carter Presidential Library. http://www.atlantafreedomtrail.com/uploads/1/0/6/4/10642571/carter_center_civil_war_history.pdf

First there are a couple of important questions I need to resolve. I knew where General Nasi had established his headquarters. It was at the old Gondar Town Hall, I'd even been inside and seen the faded paint of its entrance way. But where had the British commander, General Fowkes, positioned himself during the battle? None of the war diaries specified a location. One historical source I'd come across states that when the attacks began at dawn on Nov. 27, "Fowkes was controlling events from a battle headquarters in slit trenches at the edge of the escarpment."[94] But it doesn't say which one. After visiting many of the high points surrounding Gondar, the most prominent one I'd seen by far was Ayba Ridge. From it you could clearly see the city of Gondar little more than six miles away to the west. Besides indicating the battery's position with gun icons, the 54th Nyasaland artillery map also shows another spot close by marked OP. OP stands for "Observation Post."

On a hunch I contacted the UK's National Army Museum and asked if they had any records for Major General C.C. Fowkes. Within a couple of days, I got an email back listing several items in their collection related to the general. The second item on the list instantly caught my eye. It was a photograph whose description read "Maj Gen. C.C. Fowkes watching the battle of Gondar from battle HQ, 1941." It was followed by two more photos bearing the same description. I emailed back immediately asking if it was possible to get low-resolution copies so I could see what the photos showed. The researcher said yes, she could make reference copies with her phone. The following day I found myself looking at General Fowkes and his staff peering out intently over a line of sandbags under the spreading branches of an acacia tree. The second photo, an over-the-shoulder view, clearly shows them sitting inside a shallow trench and the steep slope of an escarpment falling away in front of them. The final photo shows the radio operator working close to the gnarled base of the acacia tree with Fowkes standing next to him either listening or dictating fresh orders. Over his shoulder is a plateau bearing a remarkable resemblance to the area of Ayba Ridge where the villagers had greeted us a few months ago. I forwarded the photos to Kebrom who quickly agreed they looked like Ayba to him. So the ridge wasn't just where my father's artillery unit was positioned. During those decisive hours of November 27, 1941, it was also

---

[94] Malcolm Page, A History of the King's African Rifles,' 2011, p. 107.

the very nerve center of the battle of Gondar, the place where the British general had his command post.

The second key question still to be resolved relates to the final climactic moments of the battle. Was Mulatu Wubneh correct about how the Wollo Banda and Mark Pilkington managed to be the first into the city and to seize General Nasi's Headquarters? It's important because the part played by the Patriot forces both at Gondar and earlier in the war to free Ethiopia has been consistently ignored or downplayed.

A few days ago, I received the translation of the final section of Gondere Bagashaw, a history of the Patriots' war by Gerima Taferes, a writer, playwright and, I discover, a Patriot fighter himself. In the final pages he tells, in dramatic, sometimes poetic language, how the Patriots lined up at dawn alongside the regular British forces for the final battle on November 27, 1941.

"Gondar was now surrounded.

Nasi's soul panicked.

The earth opened its mouth,

And grew impatient to swallow the white dishes supplied to it."[95]

Perhaps no group was more determined to serve up their Italian enemies on a plate than the Wollo Banda. For Gerima reveals a startling fact. The word *Banda*, the Italian word for band or group, had become a pejorative term. It meant "collaborators." The Patriots and the Italians themselves used it to describe the Ethiopians who fought in the colonial militias, as the Wollo had originally done.

In which case the idea that local Patriots would have joined the Wollo Banda, steering them and their British commander, Mark Pilkington, towards the quickest route to Gen. Nasi's headquarters at Fasil Ghebbi seems an unlikely one. What possible incentive would they have to help a group they viewed as enemy collaborators?

I called up Mulatu who was now back home in Silver Springs, Maryland, after completing his semester in Gondar. Together we looked to see if Gerima offers

---

[95] Gerima Taferes, 'Gondere Bagashaw,' pp. 291-93.

any alternative explanation for how Captain Pilkington and the Wollo Banda managed to be the first to reach the heart of the city.

As the regular troops of 25th infantry brigade under Brigadier James, with the Kenya armored car unit in support, advanced from the south towards Azezo, they first had to repair the damaged bridge over the Megach River. Once that was done, they ran into Nasi's most formidable remaining force, the reserve battalion under Col. Adriano Torelli. But Torelli's troops, now reduced to just two battalions, maybe 600-700 men, put up only a half-hearted resistance. As Gerima writes, "The skirmish at Azezo was not strong from the side of the enemy forces who fired sporadically." But they did slow the advance. "The retreating Italian soldiers spilled over the roads and blocked the armored cars." Which explains why Yeatman and his Kenya armored regiment were slower to reach Nasi's headquarters.[96]

Meanwhile, the Wollo Banda under Mark Pilkington weren't waiting for any bridge to be fixed. Under cover of darkness they waded across the Megach River. At dawn they attacked and quickly overran their targets for the day, the string of Italian forts defending Fantar Ridge. Spontaneously and without receiving any orders, they then charged fearlessly on towards Gondar. As Gerima describes it, they "smashed into General Martini's forces who were deployed at Addis Alem and Fit Abo. Then, they entered Gondar before the tanks which were on their way to the city via Azezo and started to hammer the Italians."

General Agostino Martini, I quickly discovered, was General Nasi's deputy, in command of the Addis Alem cavalry station. We already knew from Pilkington's letters that Addis Alem was their next target but what or where is Fit Abo?

"Oh, of course!" said Mulatu. "*Fit* means early or olden and *Abo* is short for Abune Gebremenfeskidus, an early Christian saint who's always portrayed with a long, white flowing beard and hair. Fit Abo, his church, was built by Emperor Fasilides and is one of the earliest in Gondar. It's on the old road which runs directly north from Addis Alem towards Feres Bet, which means horse barn, and then into the city." So instead of scrambling up the rough track on the hill and then through the Saturday Market, as we'd thought when we visited the area, the Wollo Banda had taken the most direct route of all. "The old caravan road," Mulatu called it, from when Gondar formed a key crossroads in Africa's overland trade

---

[96] Gerima Taferes, 'Gondere Bagashaw,' pp. 291-93.

with one road branching north towards Egypt and the other to the Arabian peninsula via the Red Sea.

Even though the Wollo Banda weren't familiar with Gondar, a burning desire to shrug off the slur of being seen as "collaborators" seems to have been what really spurred them on to be the first to reach the Castle Enclosure. There they took care of the last resistance put up by the Italian occupation forces and induced Gen. Nasi to surrender. In doing so they proved they were as worthy as any to call themselves Patriots. Even then, as Pilkington wrote later in a letter, "The credit due to them for this magnificent victory was undeservedly given to the regular forces."[97]

According to Gerima, other Patriots followed swiftly in their wake, just as Pilkington had threatened might happen, to persuade Nasi to surrender. They surged in from the West, South, and East. This growing Patriot horde, joined by ordinary citizens, converged on the Gondar radio station and destroyed it just minutes after it had broadcast General Nasi's last message: "I deem all means of further resistance exhausted."[98]

Immediately after the surrender, Gondar became a tinder box. Nasi himself called it "a volcano due to powder magazines exploding and warehouses burning." In the words of a British intelligence report, "spasmodic disorders and looting continued for several days and a number of Habash looters had to be shot."[99] The words *Habash* and *shifta* meaning bandits were often used as a derogatory term for Patriots. But Gerima suggests there were looters among the regular troops as well as the Patriots. One calming influence was Crown Prince Asfaw Wossen whom Emperor Haile Selassie in the final days had placed in command of all Patriot forces. After local merchants told him a soldier from the British forces had stolen 600,000 lire, he informed the British commander, General Fowkes. Fowkes ordered his military police to investigate, and the money was found and returned.

---

[97] Mark Pilkington, *Some Letters 1939-1942*, p. 152.

[98] Angelo Del Boca, 'Gli Italiani in Africa Orientale, Vol. 3, La caduta dell' impero, pp. 528.

[99] Adv 12A Div Intelligence Summary P.4 UK National Archives WO 276/364.

On Dec. 6th, now as provincial governor, the Crown Prince raised the Ethiopian flag at Fasilides castle and from its balcony read a statement from Haile Selassie to a jubilant crowd of Patriot fighters and ordinary people below. "You suffered incalculable losses including sacrificing your gallant fighters along the way. The flag you are watching today is, therefore, a tree of liberty that grew from the soil they ploughed and fertilized with their blood."[100]

In January 1942, Britain signed an agreement outlining the stages of its withdrawal from Ethiopia, thereby dispelling the fears of some that it intended to turn the country into a Protectorate of its own. As Churchill wrote to Haile Selassie, "Your Majesty was the first of the lawful sovereigns to be driven from his throne and country by the Fascist-Nazi criminals, and you are now the first to return in triumph."[101] Although he didn't know it, Churchill was anticipating a wave that would soon sweep across the African continent. Starting with Ghana in 1957, Britain began to grant independence to all its African colonies over the next decade.

***

On my running route this Saturday morning I've left behind the King Center and the surrounding Sweet Auburn district. I'm turning south and passing under the railroad bridge with its graffiti-covered brick supports. Emerging on the other side I see the curving granite wall surrounding Oakland Cemetery. It reminds me of the stone wall around Gondar's castles. Inside I know there are graves dating back to when my father was born in 1916 and as far back as the American Civil War.

In his book about the Patriot war, Gerima, I was surprised to find, pays poignant tribute to the role played by the 54th Nyasaland Field Battery and the other British artillery units. "On November 27 at about 6 o'clock in the morning, the order went out to fire the cannons, which were seen as the saviors of the world."

He also expresses enormous sympathy for the Nyasaland infantry men of 2/2 KAR, "who were advancing from the east to destroy the enemy stronghold at Defecha Ridge when they suddenly touched the invisible wires which triggered the

---

[100] Gerima Taferes, 'Gondere Bagashaw.' p. 296.

[101] Andrew Stewart, 'The First Victory, The Second World War and the East Africa Campaign,' 2016, Ch. 9, p. 194.

explosion of buried mines. The Ethiopians mourned their losses and wished that the explosions had taken their lives instead."[102] It seems to echo the words spoken to me by Alemu, our guard, up on that same ridge. "Your father fought alongside our fathers that day." At least 35 Malawi soldiers [then from Nyasaland] were awarded the East Africa Force Badge for bravery in Ethiopia in 1941, while dozens more were awarded the Military Medal or "mentioned in dispatches." Some of them surely died on Defecha Ridge, but others may have been among those who charged on towards its Italian fort, now under the cover of the rapid fire from the 54th Nyasaland's guns. Malawi's soldiers had in World War I already earned a reputation as having "a special aptitude for close-quarters fighting." Like the Gurkhas with their kukri knives, they would now have swarmed the Italian positions with machetes and grenades all the while screaming "Sokelai, sokelai... yao-oo-oo", their blood-curdling war cry.[103]

On Dec. 16, 1941, almost exactly a month after arriving outside Gondar, my father and the 54th Nyasaland found themselves heading to the coast to catch a ship back to the Kenyan port of Mombasa. This time he must have traveled with his spirits dramatically lifted and his outlook for the future radically changed. Perhaps my father's experience in Gondar is what inspired the enigmatic optimism that I'd seen in him in later life. That things could turn out for the best even when the future seemed portend the worst. In the Spring when he'd boarded another ship bound for Africa leaving behind an England in dire peril, with the Luftwaffe conducting nightly bombing raids on its cities, he must have wondered if he would ever be able to come home, whether England like France would be overrun and occupied by Nazi Germany. Now he and his comrades in arms were genuine heroes. Through their victory, Ethiopia became the first country to be liberated from the Axis Powers. It was an inspiring achievement at a time when things looked bleakest for the Allies in World War Two. Hitler's drive toward Moscow seemed unstoppable and the Japanese had just launched a devastating surprise attack on Pearl Harbor. By freeing Ethiopia, they also fought what was arguably the first

---

[102] Gerima Taferes, 'Gondere Bagashaw,' pp. 291-293.

[103] Timothy J. Lovering 'Authority And Identity: Malawian Soldiers in Britain's Colonial Army 1891-1964,' Doctoral Thesis U. of Sterling, pp. 253-56.

post-colonial war. This time the British had come not as conquerors but as liberators. Although Europeans like my father commanded that liberation army, they formed only a small part of it. Africans drawn from across the continent formed the vast majority of what the British historian, Andrew Stewart, describes as "a truly imperial force made up not just of different armies and air forces but of different races and religions, a microcosm of our war effort."[104] Living and working every day alongside his African gun crew, as well as the signalmen and drivers who supported them and where each man's life depended on the actions of his fellows, must have been an enlightening and inspiring experience for my father. He never shared what it meant to him, but from Mark Pilkington, a man who seems in many ways to resemble my father, I can get a sense of how he viewed his men. As Pilkington frequently wrote "the Wollo were superb, chief honour must go to them." He consistently praised their bravery and was pained by their losses.

After spending a few months regrouping in Kenya, Major Bingham informed the men of 54th Nyasaland Field Battery they had received a new assignment. They were to proceed to the Far East.[105] Their initial destination was to be Singapore but before a ship became available it fell to Japanese forces. On March 21st, 1942 they landed instead in Sri Lanka where they began preparing to fight a very different campaign in the sweltering jungles of Burma against the rapidly advancing forces of Imperial Japan. But in late 1942 my father unexpectedly, and perhaps mercifully, received new orders — he was to return to civilian life, resuming the job he'd originally been recruited for as a colonial administrator in Nyasaland. At the same time his commander, Maj. Bingham had aggravated a leg wound he'd suffered in World War I and was invalided home to England. The 54th Nyasaland Field Battery was absorbed into another East African artillery unit and along with a KAR infantry battalion from Nyasaland went on to serve with distinction in Burma. The officers of the KAR infantry again used the Malawians' reputation as fierce close-quarter fighters at least once to great effect. Their *Sokelai, Sokelai* war

---

[104] Andrew Stewart, 'The First Victory,' Ch. 5, p. 103.

[105] Maj. Francis H. Bingham, Oral History, Cat. No. 3939, Imperial War Museum, London https://www.iwm.org.uk/collections/item/object/80003923

cry echoing through trees, disorienting and striking terror into Japanese troops before they emerged screaming and wielding their deadly machetes.[106]

By the time World War II came to an end and some 28,000 Malawi soldiers began to return home,[107] my father was serving as a District Commissioner in the north of the country. I wonder if he ever ran into any of his old gun crew or other members of the 54th Nyasaland or the 2/2 KAR infantry battalion they'd fought alongside. Did he help them receive their victory medals - a pair of crossed machetes enclosed inside a wreath? Or help them with any problems they encountered getting their discharge pay? There were complaints among veterans about their treatment after the war. As one returning sergeant bluntly put it: "You say that we have done well in the war. We always hear this from Europeans, but when we return to our country you forget us, and nothing is done for us. We come back to poverty."[108] He was echoing the prophetic words of John Chilembwe, an early Malawi nationalist who died leading a failed rebellion against the British during World War I: "We have unreservedly stepped to the firing line in every conflict and played a patriot's part with the spirit of true gallantry. But in time of peace the Government failed to help the underdog. In time of peace everything is for Europeans only."[109]

Bruce Wickham continued to work in Malawi. His last position was as assistant to Kanyama Chiume, the new African Minister of Education, which he held until the country gained its independence in 1964. Which meant Africa was my home too for my first 12 years. To the casual observer, my father probably looked just like the rest of the white colonial crowd, part of the gin and gymkhana club set. But his introduction to Africa had been an unusual one, thrusting him almost immediately into a war where he fought with Africans to free another group of

---

[106] Timothy J. Lovering, 'Malawian Soldiers in Britain's Colonial Army 1891-1964,' Doctoral Thesis U. of Sterling, pp. 254-255.

[107] John McCracken, 'A History of Malawi 1859-1966,' 2012, p. 239.

[108] Timothy J. Lovering, 'Malawian Soldiers in Britain's Colonial Army 1891-1964,' Doctoral Thesis U. of Sterling, p. 289.

[109] John Chilembwe, 'The Voice of African Natives in the Present War' From 'Independent African,' by George Shepperson & Tom Price.

Africans. The month he spent in Ethiopia must have profoundly affected how he viewed the world from then on. As I grew old enough and curious enough to observe his interactions with Africans, I noticed one consistent thing: my father always spoke to them in their native language. Perhaps because it had once been so critical for communicating with his gun crew, he'd taught himself to speak it well, better in fact than all the other European adults I knew. Much later he helped me get my first real job — as translator for the Malawi embassy in Bonn, Germany — because he knew I could speak German fluently and the ambassador, Bridger Katenga, was an old friend.

***

By the time I run across Memorial Drive, heading towards Grant Park with its majestic oaks and home to the Atlanta Zoo, I pass a few dilapidated and abandoned buildings. In an overgrown yard I see a homeless encampment, one person is asleep next to a shopping cart filled with meagre belongings. It brings to mind a moment when I'm talking to Kebrom on my next to last day in Gondar. We're on the sidewalk in front of the Gondar Plaza Hotel. It's a busy upscale street. Besides the hotels, there are banks, restaurants, bars and a row of stalls selling everything from sim cards to books and clothes. There's a lot of people walking by, some relatively well off, others less so. As Kebrom and I are talking, a homeless man in shabby clothes stops right in front of me and stares at me with a strange half-smile. Kebrom and I continue to talk. Suddenly the homeless man raises his arm and starts moving it in my direction. But Kebrom's arm shoots up and blocks him and whatever he was going to do. The man shuffles away.

Kebrom is in his late 20s. I realize that in a sense he's the inheritor of the liberation that my father in a modest way helped bring about. Gondar was restored to the Gondarees. But in the eighty years since it hasn't exactly prospered. It's no longer the capital of the Amhara region. That honor was transferred to Bahir Dar, the city at the south end of Lake Tana. Mekele, the Tigrayan capital, until the recent war had far outstripped Gondar in industrial development. By most measures it's not been a winner under the ethnic federalism that governs Ethiopia. At least 25% of the young people are either unemployed or underemployed. As Kebrom told me "In your culture you have a wife, a child, a car, a house. I only have my religion. It gives me hope to live another life." And that attitude sustains him. In his Easter photo sent to me on WhatsApp, he's smiling with altar candles burning behind him.

My father was 24-years old when he went to war in Ethiopia, still at the beginning of his life in Africa. In comparison I was already 70 by the time I followed him there. During those 10 days I spent in Gondar, my main focus was on exploring a narrow window of time and space: the final campaign of World War II in Ethiopia and the vital role my father and his newly formed unit played in it. In the eighty plus years since the fighting stopped, probably noone has so painstakingly revisited this largely forgotten battleground. I was amazed at how much about my father's movements and actions I was able to uncover and relive. From the place where he and his fellow gunners fired their guns on edge of the escarpment along Ayba Ridge to the enemy's stone forts their shells struck on Defecha Ridge and up on the summit of Dunquan Hill. His thoughts and feelings about the experience still eluded me. But I could at least surmise them through others who shared his wartime experience and from the evidence I uncovered in the places he came in contact with. And by luring me to follow him and explore where he went my father gave me another priceless gift. In Ethiopia I found myself exposed to a deep well of history, culture and religion which seemed to open up to me almost at every turn. The Italians who were the enemy and occupiers had turned a centuries-old Castle Complex into the Colosseum and Forum of their new Rome in Africa. That Castle Complex had itself been built by the first Ethiopian emperor to settle in Gondar, whose architects adapted an Indian building technology brought to Ethiopia by Portuguese sailing from Goa.

Almost everything, everyone and every place in Ethiopia has a similarly intriguing chain of connections attached to it. It's a place where wars have been fought on almost the same battlefields for hundreds of years up until the very recent past as part of a never-ending struggle for power. It's also a spiritual place with hundreds active monasteries, tens of thousands of churches where attendance is over 75 percent and where one reputedly holds a mysterious object, the Ark of Covenant, believed to have resided there for well over a thousand years. It's a place of extraordinary individuals like Tewodros, the imperial Robin Hood, Ras Mikael Sehul, the calculating kingmaker and the men of the Wollo Banda, who when others called them enemy collaborators showed they could be the first to defeat the enemy. In short Ethiopia is utterly unique, a place like no other I've encountered in Africa, apart perhaps from Egypt.

At the same time Ethiopia is thoroughly African. Although I'd never been there before, everyday people, places, animals, trees, scents and smells reminded me of other African countries I'd visited and lived in during my childhood — the monkey eating its scavenged meal, the jacaranda blooming in the castle grounds, the priest and his congregation at Dunquan who invited us to share their Lenten celebration. So, for those ten days I was also on an inward-looking adventure, a time of introspection where I was trying to come to terms with what my relationship with Africa meant to me.

Significantly among the first people I told about my plan to go to Ethiopia were two of my running friends, Bill and Stan. Like me, Bill spent part of his childhood in Africa, in his case South Africa. Stan has never been to Africa but is African American and longs to go there. I'd shared with him some of my experiences growing up in Malawi. I'd even told him Nickson's story of Hlakanyana "and the yam which I found near our house" which he was afraid would never end. At some point he started referring to me as "my fellow African American." He was joking, I automatically assumed. Still, I sensed something unspoken behind the words, like "and you should be proud of it." I thought back to the dream I had of my father after I'd discovered his wartime photographs. The one where he tells me in a disconcerted tone, "I'm an odd bird, caught between two worlds." They say the people you encounter in dreams are parts of yourself. Perhaps I too am an odd bird caught between two worlds. Since my trip to Ethiopia, I've been thinking it's time for me to embrace those two worlds rather than continue to hold them apart and separate. As Stan says, I AM an African American. And a Flying One at that. In the words of South African singer Johnny Clegg, "We are the scatterlings of Africa, on a journey to the stars."

The first Ethiopian I ever encountered and wrote a film script about was called Ardi. The 137-year-old monk who blessed us at Lake Tana was a newborn compared to Ardi. He was over 4 million years old, an early hominid who lived in the Awash valley. Older even than his more famous relative Lucy.[110] The Ethiopians

---

[110] Ann Gibbons, 'A New Kind of Ancestor: Ardipithecus Unveiled,' Science 10/2/2009, Vol. 326. https://doc.rero.ch/record/211155/files/PAL_E4410.pdf

are a persistent people. Kebrom, Mulatu, Haile, Alemu, Yohannes and others I met have taught me that. If the rest of us don't destroy the planet, the odds are they will find their way to a better life. As Africans, they already know that "if you surrender to the air, you can *ride* it."

Acknowledgements

It's been over two years since my visit to Ethiopia. A few days ago, I received a WhatsApp message from Kebrom Tekle in Gondar, asking me to send a photo of him standing next to the abbot of Gorgora monastery on the shores of Lake Tana. I'm always glad to hear from Kebrom. He played such a vital and steady role in getting me to all the places I wanted to visit to relive my father's wartime experience and, in the process, became a true friend. It's also just good to know he's all right in spite of ongoing tensions across the Amhara region. Shortly after my visit, the Ethiopian Federal Government placed the province under a State of Emergency because local security forces, including the Fano militia, were refusing to disband or be absorbed into the national army. A few months later Kebrom told me that Fano had clashed with the Ethiopian National Defense Force up on Ayba Ridge, the very place where Father Abera and a crowd of Ayba villagers welcomed us and led me to the where my father's 54th Nyasaland Field Battery had dug in their guns to fight the Battle of Gondar.

Kebrom is one of the group of Ethiopians to whom I am eternally grateful for the help they gave me in making this book possible. The others are Haile Larebo who really got me started on my quest, introducing me to key individuals and pointing me to vital historical accounts of the Italian occupation, including his own. A key person Haile introduced me is Mulatu Wubneh, a Gondar native whose return there to teach a semester at the University of Gondar provided the impetus I needed to set a date and buy my plane ticket. He then played an active role in the adventure and later offered his help during several critical moments in the writing process itself. Others in Gondar to whom I am most grateful are my guards, Alemu and Yohannes, who kept me safe during our excursions to the various battle sites and two historians at the University of Gondar, Bitwoded Dagnew and Girma Tayachew, who generously shared their knowledge about the places I visited. I'm also grateful to my guide to historical sites in Gondar, Abebe Abiye, for his colorful and enlightening commentary.

Here in Atlanta, I'd like to thank my long-time friend and traveling buddy, Scott Engel, who without hesitation signed on to come with me to a place he confessed to knowing little about and immediately became captivated by. Initially, I think I failed to mention to him that it had only been a few months since a ceasefire was reached in the Civil War. To Scott I'm indebted for one of the more memorable and original insights offered in this book — *Ethiopia is the Tibet of Africa*. Also in Atlanta, I'm thankful to several members of Chattahoochee Road Runners, my running group, who cheered me on in pursuing this endeavor, in particular Stan Lane, Bill Nichols, and Dave Curry.

On the other side of Atlantic, in the UK, I'm grateful to fellow writer and documentary film veteran, Simon Mills, for his extremely valuable contribution during the research phase of my book. When the Covid lockdown was lifted Simon went to the UK National Archives and photographed a stack of military records from the Gondar Campaign that I'd identified, which included the War Diary and actual artillery map used by the 54th Nyasaland Field Battery. My thanks go also to Timothy Lovering at the University of St. Andrews in Scotland for pointing out the existence of those records in the first place and sharing his thesis on Malawian soldiers in the KAR during World War II.

During the writing process itself, I'm most indebted to Oliver Corlett, who like me was born in Malawi and went to school with me in Zimbabwe. Oliver too found his way to the United States, where Covid paradoxically brought us together even though we lived on opposite coasts. Every couple of weeks we'd meet on Zoom and discuss our thoughts on Africa past and present. Once I'd written my first draft Oliver, by then in Glasgow, Scotland, became my editor and offered invaluable comments on what was working and, more importantly, what was missing.

Once the manuscript was completed and, to my intense joy and relief, was accepted for publication by Histria Books — I'd initially presented my draft query letter to its director, Kurt Brackob, for him to critique at an Atlanta Writers Club conference — it was time to get creative again. Besides the photos, both archive and contemporary that had to be selected, I knew I also needed to provide a map, perhaps several even, to guide my readers. I quickly realized the best person to create those was a graphic artist and friend, Edmund Earle, who I'd worked with on several documentaries. Edmund had already volunteered to produce a couple of cover mock-ups for the book and now he came up with the perfect maps. They're based on the original artillery map which my father's unit had used during the battle of Gondar and which Edmund had earlier created by seamlessly joining two photographs that Simon Mills had taken of the original map held in the UK National Archives.

I'd also like to acknowledge the strong support I received during the various stages of this project from my writing community. These include Tom Chaffin, an Atlanta history writer whose most recent book *Odyssey* presents a riveting portrait of the young Charles Darwin; Richard Shirreff, author the prescient political thriller, *2017: War with Russia*, and whose father, David Shirreff's book *Bare Feet and Bandoliers*, had helped me understand the vital contribution made Ethiopian Patriot fighters in the final victory at Gondar; Aida Edemariam whose memoir, *The Wife's Tale*, about her grandmother, born in Gondar the same year as my father, painted a vivid picture of the place I was determined to visit. Aside from these, there are many authors whose works on Ethiopia and World War II history gave me crucial information and guidance in writing this book. They are listed in the bibliography section. And returning once again to Atlanta, I'd like to thank the Atlanta Writers' Club, particularly its Memoir Group which I belong to. They provided a steady source of ideas, advice and encouragement in my quest to find a publisher.

Lastly, I'd like to thank the two people who I'm closest to and who have steadfastly supported me in this five-year-long endeavor. They are my daughter, Zoë, who became the first person to read my manuscript — what better way to while away the time during a long flight to Hawaii — and my wife, Marilyn, who didn't freak out when I told her I was bent on visiting a place where a war had only just ended and who always encouraged me to follow my dream, however hard that might be, to write this, my first book.

Appendix

East Africa Command
SECRET
War Diary of 54th Nyasaland Field Battery

[Listed in UK National Archives as: East Africa: Artillery: 54 Light Battery WO 169/2980]. https://discovery.nationalarchives.gov.uk/details/r/C1003788.

Aug/Sept. 1941 Commanding Officer HF Bingham
Maj R.A.[Royal Artillery] Depot Nairobi.

29.8.41 55 African Askari from Zomba Training Centre arrived at Base Details Camp. Also 5 followers conducted to R.A. Depot, Larkhill.

30.8.41 Following officers posted. Capt. Bingham (i.c) Lt. Powis and 2nd Lts Aldous, Elliot, Sgts Leades and M/T Sgt Else attached. Three African NCOS from 53 EALB attached for duty.

31.8.41 Clothing inspection.

1.9.41 Individual training of gun layers under Officers commenced.

From 1.9. to 30.9.41 no further Europeans or Africans posted. And individual training of gun layers contd. English and Swahili lessons included in training. Lt. Powis assisted by Sgt. Loades collected stores and equipment for a 4 gun 3.7" How Bty. Rumored that Bty would be required to become an 8 gun Bty at short notice but no definite information available. Establishment not yet approved.

30.9.41 Instructed that Battery would be expanded to 8 gun unit and would be required to operate in the immediate future. Following Europeans posted. Hearn (B.Q.M.S) QMS Art Cutbush Sgts Sherman, Ramsey, Wilmore, Loades, McDonald, Wickham, Craggs posted.

30.9.41 11 Nyasa signallers from Signal School posted. 21 recruit drivers posted. 4 Signallers from Tanganyika Bty and 1 Signal Sgt and 3 Signallers from Uganda Bty.

Oct. 1941 Commanding Officer: HF Bingham Major

R.A. Depot Larkhill 1.10.41 Training contd. Source of additional personnel for Gun Detachments not decided. A/Sgt Else from R.A.S.C [service corps] promoted MT/Sgt. Posting of additional 51 African Nyasa from 13 KAR approved by 'A'.

3.10.41 Sgt Reid and Brummer posted. Vehicles drawn from V.R.D. Training contd. Sig Sgt and Signallers returned to Uganda Bty. 9 drivers posted from R.A. Depot. 2 Fitter w/ Asst. from MT dept. posted

4.10.41 Training contd. All vehicles entrained Nairobi. MT/Sgt Eales and Sgt Wickham accompanied.

7.10.41 15 recruit Drivers posted from MT Depot

8.10.41 Maj. MacCarthy I.G. [Instructor of Gunnery] and TSM Goode attached and to accompany 4 Drivers posted from R.A. Depot and 7 recruit drivers posted from MT Depot. 16 Non-combatant EAMLS posted from 55th and 56th Btys

9.10.41 Arrangements made personally with O.C. 13 KAR for 51 Askari to be transferred to 54 Bty. on Oct. 12

12.10.41 Orders to move 13 Oct. 2/Lt Tomlinson posted.

13.10.41 I L/Bdr and 51 Askari of 13 KAR taken over at Base Detail Camp. Battery less advanced party and vehicles entrained and left Nairobi at 1100 hrs.

Capt. Strother-Stewart and Lt. Tucker joined. Also 2 Dressers EARAMC and 3 Nyasa signallers from Signal School.

14:10:41 Arrive Kilindini 0600 hrs. Immediately embarked. Sailed 11.45

At Sea 15-16.10.41 Troops suffering severely from seasickness. Boat drills. Training impossible.

17.10.41 Arrived Mogadishu. 2/Lt Block. Sgt. Percival and 17 gunners from 53 EALB joined. Also 1 Cook, 1 Sweeper and 1 Servant. Sailed same day.

18.10.41 Troops beginning to recover from seasickness. Signallers continued training. Gun layers classes with Dial Sights and Sight Clinometers. Lewis gun classes.

20.10.41 Training contd. Classes for officers and BNCOs and Minature[sic] Range held by I.G.

23.10.41 Arrival in Aden in evening about 1830 hrs.

24.10.41 Gunners David Moses and Dawa admitted to hospital. Sailed from Aden 1400.

25-28.10.41 Training contd. I.G.s classes for European personnel contd.

Massawa 29.10.41 Arrived in Massawa at noon. Disembarked and spent night there. Vehicles already arrived and unloaded.

Asmara 30.10.41 26 Drivers of Cape Corps reported Massawa to assist drive vehicles. Battery leaves Massawa for Asmara. All in at 2300. Capt. Strother-Stewart's staff truck giving trouble. Camped at East African Details camp.

31.10.41 Vehicle maintenance. Kit inspections. Medical inspections. Incidence of V.D. very high. Cases contracted immediately before leaving East Africa. Very cold. Bad camp and no proper sanitation.

Nov. 1941 Commanding Officer: HF Bingham Major

Asmara 1.11.41 Signal equipment overhauled. Battery organized into troops. Load tables etc prepared.

2.11.41 Sunday. No training.

3.11.41 Training w/o guns. Collected and sorted 1536 runs of ammunition.

6.11 Full ammunition echelon 1536 rounds collected from ammunition dump.

10.11.41 Maj. McCarthy & Lt. Tucker and advance party left w/ 3 vehicles for forward area to survey battle positions.

11.11.41 Heard ship w/ guns docking in Massawa that day. Left w/ gun 'towers' [trucks that tow] at 2:45pm. Capt. Lewis and 'B' Echelon [B troop?] under

Capt. Powis instructed to leave for forward area 11.12. Arranged for Cape Corps relief drivers to wait Adowa.

Arrived at Massawa 6pm but ship didn't arrive that night.

Massawa 12.11.41 Ship docked at 7am. Discovered 25pounders loaded behind 18/25 pounders [older model].

12.11 [contd.] Unloading very slow because of 'no proper gear', took till 4pm. No documentation with boxes of gun stores. Arrived at Asmara at 11:30 at night. Trouble with one 'tower.' Met by Lt. Jessup OME [engineers?] Decided to pull guns into Ordnance Workshop at 6am following morning.

Asmara 13.11.41 2 Sight inclinometers broken unloading. One gun required replacement pressure pump, flown in from Khartoum that evening. Guns also spray painted.

14.11.41 8:45am left Asmara, camped 72 miles beyond Adowa.

15.11.41 Proceeded by Ad Arcai road to foot of Wolchefit Escarpment. 'Gun towers badly in need of rest after 9 hours pulling over incredible mountain roads.' Found B Echelon ammunition truck w/ cracked cylinder head.

16.11.41 Battery started up Wolchefit Escarpment at dawn, 'stupendous but gradients reasonable'. Battery reached top by 8am without incident. Proceeded to report for orders and met 'C.R.A' [Col Ormsby] near Debat. Camped for night at Km 497 on Gondar road and instructed by 'Div: General' [Lt-Gen Fowkes] 'to be in action the following day.'

17.11.41 Moved into position behind Argiv Ridge. Established 2 O.P.s [See Artillery Map] First round fired by 'A' at 14:30 Hrs. CRA [Commander, Royal Artillery Col. J. Ormsby present at O.P.

18.11.41 Enemy positions on Ambazzo, Larei and Crescent Hill engaged and targets registered. [Capture of Venticinque] Congratulatory telegram received from C.R.A. and communicated to all ranks. Sgt. Sharman posted from 53rd EALB. Night firing.

19.11.41 Targets of opportunity engaged. Shooting satisfactory. 'A' Sub gun out of action. Recuperator leaking from plug in rear of high pressure cylinder. Gun evacuated to No. 2 workshop.

20.11.41 Practice shooting contd. Div: Gen [Fowkes] visited O.P. 'A' Gun stripped and recuperator evacuated to Ordnance Asmara.

21.11.41 Firing contd from same positions. Some shelling of O.P. No damage or casualties. Battery position never engaged by enemy.

22.11.41 Firing contd. 'A' Gun's recuperator arrived from Asmara still leaking. Ordnance Artificer in field workshop tackled the job himself and 10lb solder put into plug.

23.11.41 Firing contd. From same position. 'A' gun in action. Repairs apparently satisfactory.

24.11.41 Firing contd in same position

25.11.41 'B' Troop moved to battle position in rear of McLean's O.P. [On Map Campbell's OP?] 'B' Troop in position by 1700. 'A' Troop remained in old position and continued firing

26.11.41 'A' Troop fired 2 salvos at 0815 and then moved to battle position. In position at 1200. Registered targets on Deflecha Ridge, Maldiba and Deva at 1730. Enemy fire few rounds near O.P. at dusk. No casualties.

27:11:41 Attack on Gondar. Opened at 0530 Hrs. Harrassing fire on Deflecha Ridge by 'A' Troop. 'B' Troop on Maldiba. Capt. Strother-Stewart F.O.O. with Sgt. Reid. F.O.O. party forward to Gantz Hill [See Artillery Map] Wireless communication interrupted by jamming. Line broken in several places. Wireless communication through 11.00 hrs. 10:45 Campbell of 22nd Mountain Bty called for supporting fire on southern Deflecha Ridge as infantry up in that area. 76 rounds fired in 6 minutes [9-10 per gun] and shoot entirely successful as enemy abandoned entire position setting fire to ammunition dump. 'A' Troop engaged enemy guns on Deva whenever these opened and prevented them giving continuing support to their own infantry. Observation very difficult as guns cleverly sited on edge of wooded ravine. Also withdrawn into tunnels whenever we opened fire. Report from infantry via 22 Mountain Bty that enemy guns beyond Gondar firing onto forward infantry and causing them some annoyance. Enemy guns located on crest of Dunquan Hill, map range 15,500 yds. [See Artillery Map] Guns engaged and silenced after 19 rounds had been fired by 'A' Troop. These guns did not fire again during the action. Enemy did not try to engage either the O.P. or Battery position throughout the action.

28.11.41 'A' Troop moved to position O.P. 3. [See Artillery Map] Line reeled in. 'B' Troop followed. 'A' Troop in position by 1200 hrs. 'B' Troop in position by 1530.

29.11.41 At O.P.3 maintenance of Guns and equipment; Wireless tender from Div: Sigs attached. During the morning white flags seen on Deva and Ambazzo

30.11.41 Remained at O.P. 3. Make and mend. Maintenance of signal equipment. No 18 damaged and written off after being run over by lorry.

Dec. 1941 Commanding Officer: HF Bingham Major

Field. 1.12.41 Battery moved to Kilometer 499 on Gondar Rd., 21 miles from Gondar. Bitterly cold but men seem to stand up to it extraordinarily well. Incidence of sickness surprisingly low.

2.12.41 Individual training commenced. Signal section formed under Sgt. Ramsey for instruction. Layers classes and Lewis Gun classes.

3.12.41 Individual Training contd.

4.12.41 Maj. MacCarthy ceased to be attached and left the unit for return to Nairobi. Training cont. 2/Lt Durie posted from 51st (G.C.) Light Battery.

5.12.41 Training cont

6.12.41 Kit inspection and Gun Park inspection

7.12.41 Church parade. Parties all denominations to Gondar for divine service.

8.12.41 Training cont. 'A' Gun could not be pulled back. Recuperator stripped by Sgt. Wilmore. Recuperator cylinder flew out due to aeration in oil. Floating piston hopelessly jammed. Have t call in C.O.M.E. Capt Strother-Stewart and Lt. Tucker left unit on return to Gold Coast.

9.12.41 C.O.M.E unable to effect satisfactory repair to recuperator 'A' Gun. New recuperator will probably be required. Individual training cont. Progress of new layers satisfactory.

10-11.12.41 Training cont.

p.2 12-13.12.41 Individual training cont.

14.12.41 Church parade in Gondar. Lt. Connaughton joined from 51 G.C. Light Bty

15.12.41 Drill order with 'A' Troop. Occupation of position. 17:25 Instruction from Brigade that Battery required to move at once and proceed to Massawa to embark for East Africa.

16.12.41 Left Km 499 0800hrs. Camped at Adi Arcai. Considerable trouble with MT

17.12.41 Left Adi Arcai 0830. B.C. went on to Asmara for instructions. Battery camped at Adowa. More trouble with MT.

18.12.41 Left Adowa 0800. Battery all in Asmara by 1530 except 3 Ton Lorry on tow.

19.12.41 Leaving 3 ton lorry in Asmara for repairs. Battery proceeded without incident to Massawa and camped in transit camp.

20.12.41 At Massawa awaiting transport. 10 BNCOs attached from 53rd Bty for return to Depot.

21.12.41 Capt. Powis with 3 officers 6 BNCOs and 91 African Ranks embarked H.M.T Dunera. Sailed afternoon 22 Dec

23.12.41 Maj. Bingham with 'A' Troop and Drivers and attached BNCOs sailed H.M.T Llandaff Castle. Strength 4 Officers, 16 BNCOs and 172 African ranks. 5 Staff trucks handed over to Movement 'Q' for loading on S.S. Palermo.

p.3 24-25.12.41 Boat stations and roll call parade

26.12.41 Arrived Berbera. 800 Italian Political Refugees embarked. Gunners undertook all guard duties.

27-31.12.41 At sea. Guard duties.

54th Nyasaland Artillery Map

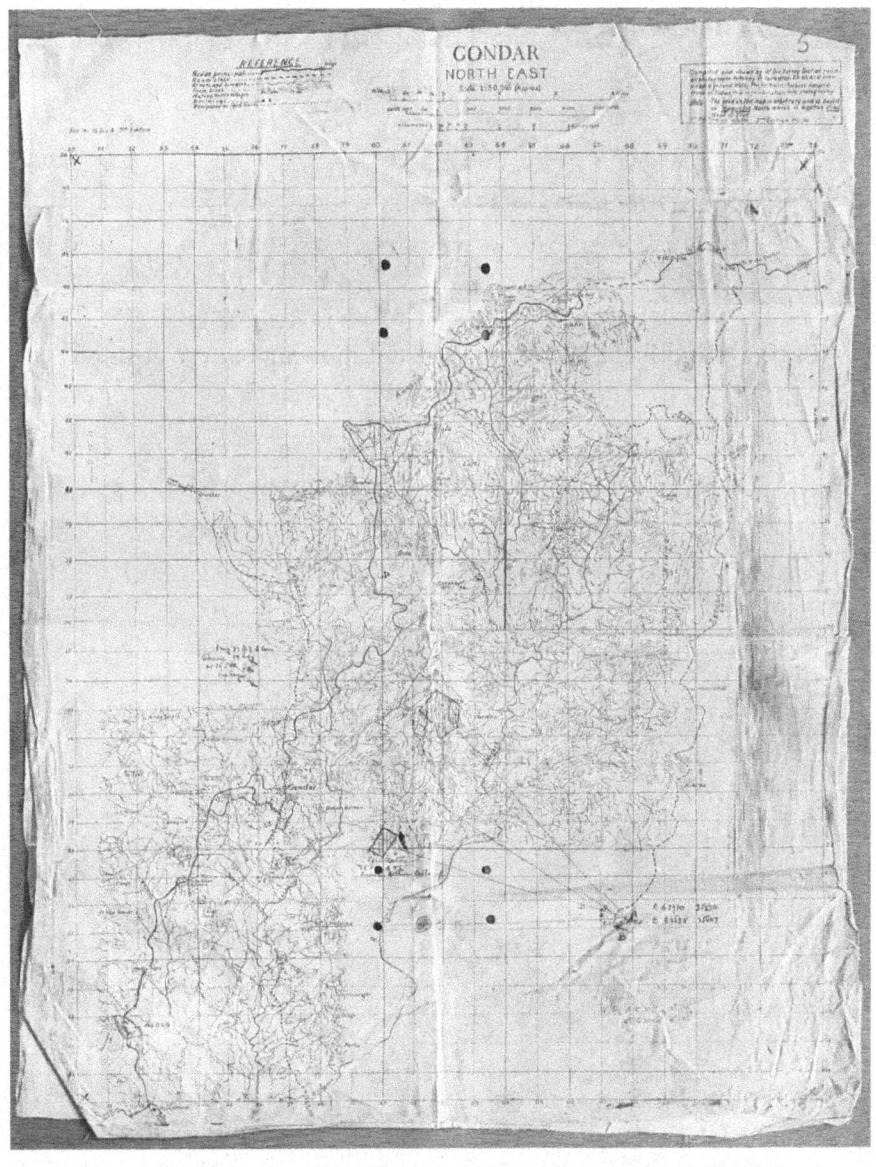

54th Nyasaland Field Battery map for Battle of Gondar

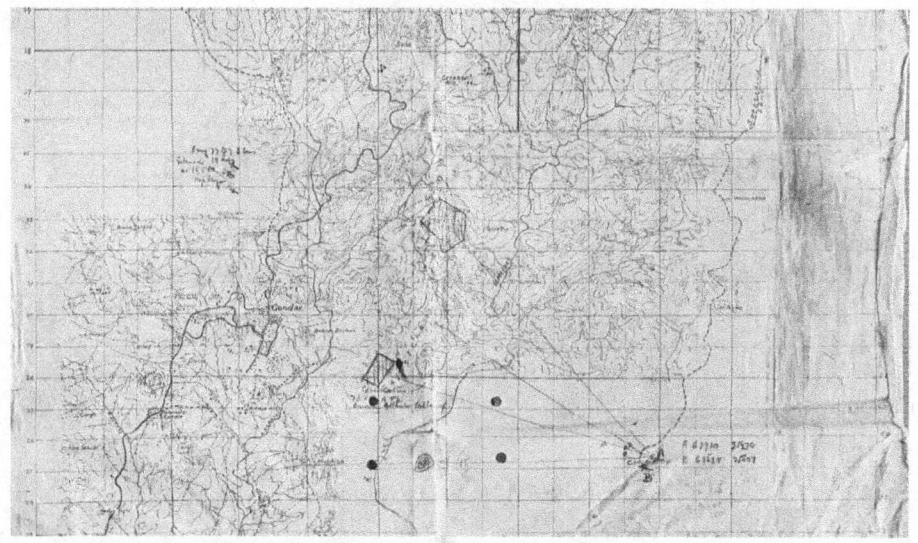

54th Nyasaland Field Battery map, detail showing battery position and target lines

Maps Credit: UK National Archives

Select Bibliography

Bahru Zewde. *A History of Modern Ethiopia, 1855-1991*. Ohio University Press, 2002.

Blundell, Michael. *A Love Affair with the Sun: a Memoir of Seventy Years in Kenya*. Kenway Publications, 1994.

Bruce, James *Travels to Discover the Source of the Nile*. (1790 edition), Vol. 2, Book 4, Vol. 3, Books 5 & 8

Del Boca, Angelo *Gli Italiani in Africa Orientale*, Vol. 2, *La conquista dell' impero'* Mondadori, 2014.

Edemariam, Aida, *The Wife's Tale: A Personal History*, Harper, 2018.

Gerima Taferes, *Gondere Bagashaw* [Amharic] (2nd publication) Far East Printing Press: Addis Ababa, 2008 (E.C.).

Haile M. Larebo, *The Building of an Empire : Italian Land Policy and Practice in Ethiopia, 1935-1941*. Red Sea Press, 2006 [Oxford U. Press, 1994].

Lovering, Timothy J. *Authority And Identity: Malawian Soldiers in Britain's Colonial Army, 1891-1964*. Doctoral Thesis, Dept. of History, U. of Sterling, 2002.

Mark Pilkington: Some Letters 1939-1942. Privately published, 1947.

Marcus, Harold G. *A History of Ethiopia*. U. of California Press, 2002.

Morrison, Toni. *Song of Solomon*. Vintage, 2004.

Moyse-Bartlett, Lt-Col. Hubert *The King's African Rifles*, Vol. 2, Naval & Military Press, 2016. And on Google Books https://play.google.com/books/reader?id=aHC-BAAAQBAJ&pg=GBS.PP1

Mulatu Wubneh, "Urban resilience and sustainability of the city of Gondar (Ethiopia) in the face of adverse historical changes," *Planning Perspectives Journal*, Vol. 36, 2021 Issue 2 https://www.tandfonline.com/doi/full/10.1080/02665433.2020.1753104

Page, Malcolm *King's African Rifles: A History*. Pen & Sword, 2011.

Pankhurst, Richard *History of Ethiopian Towns From the Mid-19th Century to 1935*. Wiesbaden: Steiner, 1982.

Pankhurst, Richard *The Ethiopian Borderlands: Essays in Regional History from Ancient Times to the End of the 18th Century*. Red Sea Press, 1997.

Playfair, Maj-Gen. I.S.O. *History of the Second World War 'The Mediterranean and the Middle East' Vol. 1 The Early Success against Italy (to May 1941)*. United Kingdom Military Series, 1954.

Ch. VI. Italy Declares War, pp. 109-124.
Ch. IX. The First Encounters on the Borders of Italian East Africa, pp. 165-184.
Ch. XXI. The Italians lose the initiative in East Africa, pp. 391-406.
Ch. XXII. The Advance to Addis Ababa through Somalia and Gojjam, pp. 407-428.
Ch. XXIII. Victory On The Northern Front In East Africa, pp.429-449.
https://archive.org/details/mediterranean-middle-east-vol-1.

Playfair, Maj-Gen. I.S.O. *History of the Second World War: The Mediterranean and the Middle East Vol. 2 The Germans Come Help Their Ally (1941)*. United Kingdom Military Series, 1956, Ch. XVI The Final Campaign in East Africa, pp. 303-323. https://www.ibiblio.org/hyperwar/UN/UK/UK-Med-II/.

Pearce, Jeff *Prevail: The Inspiring Story of Ethiopia's Victory over Mussolini's Invasion*. Skyhorse Publishing, 2014.

Shirreff, David *Bare Feet and Bandoliers: Wingate, Sandford, the Patriots and the Liberation of Ethiopia*. Pen & Sword Military, 2009.

Poncet, Charles-Jacques. *The Red Sea and Adjacent Countries at the close of the 17th Century*, edited by William Foster. The Hakluyt Society, 1949.

Stewart, Andrew. *First Victory: The Second World War and the East Africa Campaign*. Yale University Press, 2016.

The Jesuits in Ethiopia (1609-1641): Latin Letters in Translation. Edited by Wendy Belcher, Chronology & Introduction by Leonardo Cohen, Harrassowitz Verlag, 2017.

About the Author

Jonathan Wickham was born in Malawi, in southern Africa, educated in the UK and has spent most of his career in the US producing documentaries for television. He works primarily as a scriptwriter, taking complex subjects from science, history and contemporary life and fashioning them into dramatic character-driven stories. His programs have aired on leading national and local broadcast channels. He has received a Southeast Emmy award for best documentary. He's also written magazine articles for Georgia Historical Quarterly and Georgia Backroads. *Ten Days That Shook My World* is his first book.

HISTRIA BOOKS

HISTRIA PERSPECTIVES

BOOKS THAT CHALLENGE AND ENLIGHTEN

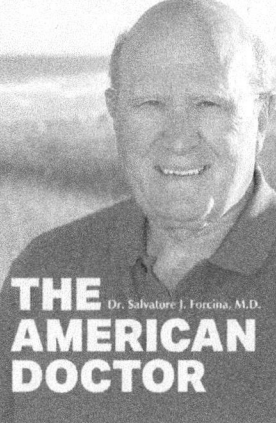

FOR THESE AND OTHER GREAT BOOKS VISIT
HistriaBooks.com